Travel Guide 2025

The Island of the Ancients, Bora Bora, Moorea, Raiatea & Huahine, Marquesas Islands, Traditions and Festivals.

Pamala Whitney

Copyright © 2024. All rights reserved. Pamala Whitney

No part of this publication may be reproduced, distributed, or transmitted in any form or by any means, including photocopying, recording, or other electronic or mechanical methods, without the prior written permission of the publisher, except in the case of brief quotations embodied in critical reviews and certain other noncommercial uses permitted by copyright law.

This book is a work of nonfiction. The author has made every effort to ensure the accuracy of the information presented at the time of publication. However, the author and publisher assume no responsibility for errors, omissions, or changes in details that may occur after publication.

Trademark Disclaimer: All product names, logos, brands, and other trademarks mentioned or referred to within this book are the property of their respective trademark holders. Use of these names, logos, and brands does not imply endorsement or affiliation. All trademarks mentioned are used for identification purposes only and remain the property of their respective owners.

This disclaimer protects you in case you reference any branded names or logos in your book, making it clear that you don't claim ownership or imply any official partnership.

Table of Contents

Chapter 1. Introduction — 7
- Overview of Tahiti & French Polynesia — 7
- Why Visit: Unique Features of Tahiti & French Polynesia — 8

Chapter 2. Top Islands to Visit — 10
- Tahiti — 10
- Bora Bora — 12
- Moorea — 16
- Raiatea & Huahine — 19
- Huahine: The Island of the Ancients — 21
- Marquesas Islands — 23

Chapter 3. Beaches and Natural Wonders — 28
- Iconic Beaches — 28
- Haapiti Beach (Moorea) — 29
- Poe Beach (Tahiti) — 29
- Coral Reefs and Lagoon Exploration — 30
- Waterfalls and Hiking Trails — 32

Chapter 4. Top Attractions — 38
- Polynesian Cultural Center — 38
- Fautaua Waterfall — 39
- Bora Bora Lagoon — 40
- Black Sand Beaches (Tahiti & French Polynesia) — 41

Chapter 5. History & Culture — 42
- Ancient Polynesian History — 42
- Tahitian Traditions and Festivals — 43
- Local Arts, Music, and Dance — 45

Chapter 6. Local Cuisine — 47
- Traditional Dishes to Try — 47
- Dining Recommendations — 48

Chapter 7. Accommodation — 51
- Luxury Resorts — 51
- Budget Stays — 52
- Eco-Friendly Options — 53

Chapter 8. Things to Do — 55
- Adventure Activities: Snorkeling, Diving, Hiking — 55
- Relaxation: Spas, Beaches, and Lagoon Cruises — 59
- Cultural Experiences: Traditional Craft Workshops, Festivals — 62

Chapter 9. Practical Information — 65
- Best Time to Visit — 65

Getting Around the Islands	67
Ferry Services for Day Trips and Tours	71
Getting Around the Islands	72
Safety and Health Tips	75
Chapter 10. Day Trips and Excursions	**79**
Exploring Neighboring Islands	79
Must-See Hidden Gems	80
Bonus	80
Useful website	81

Chapter 1. Introduction

Overview of Tahiti & French Polynesia

Tahiti and French Polynesia have always felt like the epitome of a tropical paradise, a place where the world slows down, and every moment is a blend of natural beauty and rich culture. From the moment I first laid eyes on these islands, I was struck by their breathtaking landscapes—turquoise waters meeting lush, green mountains, framed by delicate palm trees swaying in the breeze. It's a place where the horizon stretches endlessly, and the sky turns into a masterpiece at sunset.

Tahiti, the largest and most populous island, is often the gateway to French Polynesia. Its vibrant capital, Papeete, offers a mix of modern life and traditional Polynesian charm, where you can explore local markets, dine on fresh seafood, and admire the colorful, handcrafted goods. Yet, even here, the island's natural beauty takes center stage—the towering peaks of the island's volcanic mountains offer hiking opportunities with stunning views, and the lagoons surrounding the island are perfect for snorkeling.

But it's the islands beyond Tahiti that make French Polynesia a truly magical destination. Bora Bora, with its picture-perfect overwater bungalows, is often called the "Pearl of the Pacific." Here, crystal-clear waters with vibrant coral reefs make it a haven for divers and beach lovers alike. Moorea, just a short boat ride from Tahiti, enchants with its jagged mountain ridges and quiet, secluded beaches. Each island in French Polynesia offers a unique blend of beauty, from the cultural richness of Raiatea to the untouched wilderness of the Marquesas.

For me, what makes Tahiti and French Polynesia so special is the deep sense of tranquility that pervades the islands. Whether you're strolling through a quiet village, watching traditional Tahitian dance, or simply enjoying the warm sun on the beach, there's a peacefulness here that's hard to find elsewhere in the world. But it's also the people—the Polynesians—whose warmth and hospitality leave a lasting impression. They share their culture, traditions, and history with pride, making you feel not just like a visitor, but a welcomed part of their world.

Tahiti and French Polynesia are not just a destination, but a journey into the heart of the Pacific, where the beauty of nature and the richness of culture come together in a way that feels timeless. Whether you're here for adventure, relaxation, or cultural exploration, these islands promise an experience that will stay with you forever.

Why Visit: Unique Features of Tahiti & French Polynesia

Tahiti and French Polynesia are more than just a collection of islands—they're an invitation to experience a world that feels both familiar and exotic, where nature, culture, and adventure converge in the most captivating way. The allure of these islands is undeniable, and there are so many unique features that make them a must-visit destination for any traveler. Here are just a few of the reasons why these islands are worth the journey:

Unmatched Natural Beauty The landscapes here are like something out of a dream. From Tahiti's lush green mountains to Bora Bora's sparkling turquoise lagoons, the natural beauty of these islands is beyond compare. Picture-perfect beaches, towering waterfalls, and coral reefs teeming with marine life—there's no shortage of breathtaking scenery around every corner. Whether you're hiking through rainforests, swimming with rays and sharks, or simply lounging on the sand, the landscape feels like it was designed for relaxation and exploration.

World-Class Beaches The beaches of French Polynesia are iconic, and many of them are often considered among the best in the world. Bora Bora's famed Matira Beach, with its soft white sand and clear blue waters, is a prime example of paradise. Moore's secluded coves and Tahiti's black sand beaches offer something for every kind of beach lover. These beaches are perfect for lounging, swimming, snorkeling, and sunbathing, and with such pristine, untouched shores, you'll feel like you've discovered your own slice of heaven.

Rich Polynesian Culture French Polynesia is steeped in culture and history. From the sacred rituals of the islands to the vibrant art and music, there's a deep sense of tradition that runs through everyday life. The

Polynesian people are incredibly welcoming and eager to share their customs with visitors. You'll find traditional dance performances, vibrant festivals, and art forms like tattooing and weaving that have been passed down for generations. This rich cultural tapestry gives visitors a deeper understanding of life on these islands, making your trip more than just a holiday, but a journey into the heart of Polynesian heritage.

Unique Marine Life The waters around Tahiti and the surrounding islands are home to some of the most diverse marine ecosystems in the world. Snorkeling and diving here are unparalleled, offering opportunities to swim with sea turtles, rays, colorful fish, and even sharks. The crystal-clear lagoons and coral reefs are teeming with life, making it a diver's dream. The opportunity to explore the underwater world of French Polynesia is one of the most exciting and unique aspects of a visit to these islands.

Luxurious Yet Accessible Accommodations French Polynesia offers a wide range of accommodations, from overwater bungalows in Bora Bora to charming beachfront villas in Moorea. The overwater bungalow experience, where you can sleep just steps away from the turquoise waters, is a hallmark of luxury here. But beyond the luxury, there are plenty of options for all budgets, with eco-friendly resorts and budget-friendly guesthouses available on many islands. It's the perfect place to indulge in luxury without sacrificing accessibility or comfort.

Exclusivity and Serenity Unlike other tourist hotspots, Tahiti and French Polynesia remain relatively unspoiled. The islands are less crowded, offering a serene atmosphere that makes it easy to escape the hustle and bustle of daily life. Whether you're in a bustling market in Papeete or relaxing on a remote beach, the lack of mass tourism allows for an experience that feels intimate and special. This makes it a perfect destination for those seeking both adventure and quiet relaxation in an idyllic setting.

Adventure Awaits If you're someone who loves adventure, French Polynesia offers a treasure trove of activities. From hiking in the volcanic mountains of Tahiti to paddleboarding on the calm waters of Moorea's lagoons, the outdoor opportunities are endless. Kayaking, deep-sea fishing, sailing, and even exploring ancient Polynesian archaeological sites will keep the most active traveler entertained.

Tahiti and French Polynesia offer an experience like no other, where you can immerse yourself in the natural beauty, culture, and adventure of one of the most unique places on earth. Whether you're looking for relaxation, exploration, or cultural enrichment, these islands promise to leave you with unforgettable memories.

Chapter 2.Top Islands to Visit

Tahiti

Tahiti: The Heart of French Polynesia

Tahiti, the largest and most populous island in French Polynesia, is the gateway to the paradise that lies beyond. Known for its dramatic landscapes, bustling capital, and rich cultural heritage, Tahiti offers visitors a unique blend of relaxation, adventure, and cultural immersion. Whether you're looking to hike through verdant valleys, explore volcanic mountains, or experience the lively rhythm of Tahitian life, Tahiti has something for every traveler.

What to Explore in Tahiti

Papeete: The Vibrant Capital Papeete, the capital city of Tahiti, is where modern life meets traditional Polynesian culture. The city is a vibrant hub for shopping, dining, and cultural experiences. Be sure to visit the Papeete Market, where you can browse local handicrafts, fresh produce, and traditional Tahitian goods. The market is a great place to pick up souvenirs like Tahitian pearls and hand-woven baskets. Additionally, Papeete's waterfront is lined with restaurants and cafes offering stunning views of the ocean and nearby islands.

The Island's Beaches Tahiti's beaches may not have the iconic white sand like Bora Bora or Moorea, but they are still stunning in their own right. The island's black sand beaches, formed by volcanic eruptions, are both unique and picturesque. Plage de Toaroto and Plage de Maui are two popular beaches where you can relax or snorkel in the calm waters.

Fautaua Waterfall A must-see for nature lovers, the Fautaua Waterfall is one of the tallest waterfalls in French Polynesia, cascading 300 meters down from the island's volcanic mountains. It's an adventurous hike to reach the waterfall, offering sweeping views of the island and lush tropical surroundings.

Mount Orohena If you're a hiking enthusiast, a trek up Mount Orohena, the highest point in Tahiti, is a rewarding experience. The hike can take anywhere from 5 to 8 hours, depending on your fitness level, but the panoramic views of the island and ocean from the summit are absolutely worth the effort.

Tahiti Iti The smaller peninsula of Tahiti Iti, located at the southeastern tip of the island, offers a quieter and more secluded escape. Here, you can explore pristine beaches, walk through tropical forests, and visit traditional villages. Teahupo'o, on the southern coast of Tahiti Iti, is famous for its world-class surf breaks, attracting surfers from around the world.

Cultural Experiences Tahiti is a place where you can connect with the island's Polynesian culture. Attend a traditional Tahitian dance performance, visit the Museum of Tahiti and Her Islands to learn about the history of the region, or explore Marae temples, ancient Polynesian sites used for religious ceremonies. The Heiva Festival in July is also an excellent opportunity to experience local music, dance, and cultural exhibitions.

How to Get to Tahiti

By Air:
The main international gateway to Tahiti is Faa'a International Airport (PPT), located just outside of Papeete. Direct flights to Tahiti are available from major cities in the Pacific, Asia, the United States, and New Zealand. Common direct flights include:

- Los Angeles (LAX) to Tahiti: Approximately 8 hours.
- Auckland (AKL) to Tahiti: Approximately 5.5 hours.
- Paris (CDG) to Tahiti: Approximately 22 hours (with a layover, typically in Los Angeles).

Once in Tahiti, you can take domestic flights to nearby islands like Bora Bora, Moorea, and Huahine, or explore the island by car or taxi.

By Boat:
Cruise ships also frequent Tahiti, offering passengers the chance to explore the island and the rest of

French Polynesia. Tahiti's Port of Papeete is a popular stop for large cruise lines, with departures from various international ports.

Cost of Visiting Tahiti Tahiti is known for being a more expensive destination, but costs can vary depending on your style of travel.

Flights:

- Round-trip flights from Los Angeles to Tahiti generally range from $600 to $1,200 depending on the season. Flights from Paris or New Zealand can be more expensive, typically around $1,200 to $2,000.

Accommodation:
Accommodation options in Tahiti range from budget to luxury:

- Budget hotels and guesthouses: $70 to $150 per night.
- Mid-range hotels: $150 to $300 per night.
- Luxury resorts (including overwater bungalows): $300 to $1,500+ per night.

Food and Dining:

- Street food and casual dining: $10 to $20 per meal.
- Mid-range restaurants: $25 to $50 per meal.
- Fine dining: $50+ per person.

Activities:

- Hiking, visiting cultural sites, and beach activities are usually free or low-cost.
- Guided tours, water sports, and snorkeling excursions can range from $50 to $150 depending on the activity.
- A diving session can cost around $100 to $200.

Transportation:

- Public buses in Papeete are affordable, costing around $1 to $2 per ride.
- Taxis can be more expensive, with fares starting around $15 to $20 for short trips.
- Renting a car can cost $40 to $80 per day.

Tahiti is an island that offers much more than just its beautiful beaches—it's a place where you can immerse yourself in a rich cultural heritage, explore stunning natural landscapes, and experience a peaceful, welcoming atmosphere. While it may not be the cheapest destination, the memories and experiences you'll take away from this unique island will be worth every penny. Whether you're visiting for relaxation, adventure, or cultural discovery, Tahiti promises an unforgettable journey.

Bora Bora

Bora Bora: The Pearl of the Pacific

Bora Bora, often referred to as the "Pearl of the Pacific," is the embodiment of tropical paradise. Known for its turquoise lagoons, lush green mountains, and overwater bungalows, Bora Bora has long been a dream destination for travelers seeking luxury, romance, and adventure. It's the kind of place where every corner looks like a postcard, and the vibrant underwater world and stunning landscapes are simply breathtaking.

What to Explore in Bora Bora

Bora Bora Lagoon The crown jewel of Bora Bora is its lagoon, a vast stretch of crystal-clear water encircling the island. The lagoon is home to an incredible diversity of marine life, making it one of the top spots in the world for snorkeling and diving. The Coral Gardens, located near the main island, are especially popular for snorkeling, where visitors can swim alongside colorful fish, rays, and sea turtles. The lagoon is also a favorite for romantic boat cruises, where you can enjoy the views of the island's lush peaks while sipping a tropical drink.

Mount Otemanu Mount Otemanu, the highest point in Bora Bora, is a dormant volcano that offers adventurous travelers a challenging hike with panoramic views of the island and lagoon below. The trek is a bit strenuous but incredibly rewarding, as you'll pass through dense tropical jungle and discover dramatic cliffs and valleys. Reaching the summit provides a once-in-a-lifetime opportunity to experience Bora Bora's stunning landscape from above.

Matira Beach Matira Beach is one of Bora Bora's most famous and accessible beaches, offering soft white sand and shallow, calm waters perfect for swimming. It's also the perfect spot for a romantic sunset stroll, with a view of the island's jagged peaks and the vibrant colors of the evening sky reflecting off the water. The beach has a relaxed vibe and a few restaurants nearby where you can sample local cuisine while enjoying the sea breeze.

Lagoon Tours and Shark & Ray Snorkeling One of the best ways to explore Bora Bora's lagoon is by taking a boat tour, many of which include shark and ray snorkeling. On these tours, you'll have the opportunity to swim with blacktip sharks, rays, and other marine life in the crystal-clear waters of the lagoon. These tours offer a unique, close-up experience with some of the ocean's most fascinating creatures, all while being guided by local experts.

Bora Bora's Vaitape Village Vaitape, the main village on Bora Bora, is a charming spot to explore local life. Here, you can visit the market to buy fresh produce, handcrafted goods, and local souvenirs, or stop by one of the island's cafes for a taste of French Polynesian cuisine. Vaitape also offers a chance to see the island's cultural history, including remnants of old temples (marae) and war memorials from World War II.

Overwater Bungalows While not a specific location to explore, the overwater bungalows that many of Bora Bora's luxury resorts offer are a signature feature of the island. Staying in one of these private, elevated bungalows allows you to experience Bora Bora's beauty in a truly unique way. You can watch tropical fish swimming beneath your feet as you sip your morning coffee or enjoy a sunset cocktail while overlooking the lagoon. It's a dream experience that many visitors come to Bora Bora specifically to enjoy.

Mt. Pahia Summit

Bora Bora
Famed resort islands
with a barrier reef

Bora Bora

Scan the QR code

1. **Open Camera:** Launch your smartphone's camera app.
2. **Position QR Code:** Place the QR code within the camera's viewfinder.
3. **Hold Steady:** Keep the device steady for the camera to focus.
4. **Wait for Scan:** Wait for the code to be recognized.
5. **Tap Notification:** Follow the prompt to access the content.

How to Get to Bora Bora

13

- **By Air:** Bora Bora is accessible via Motu Mute Airport (BOB), located on a small islet just off the main island. To get there, most travelers fly into Faa'a International Airport (PPT) in Tahiti (the capital of French Polynesia) and then take a short domestic flight to Bora Bora, which lasts about 50 minutes. There are daily flights to Bora Bora from Tahiti, operated by Air Tahiti.
- Flights from Los Angeles (LAX) to Papeete (PPT) typically take around 8 hours, and from there, you'll catch a connecting flight to Bora Bora. You can also reach Bora Bora by boat from Tahiti, although it's a longer journey.
- **By Boat:** Cruise ships also frequent Bora Bora, often as part of a French Polynesia itinerary. Bora Bora's Vaitape Port welcomes cruises, and docking here provides an excellent opportunity to explore the island's beauty at a more leisurely pace.

Cost of Visiting Bora Bora

Bora Bora is known for being a high-end luxury destination, but it offers a variety of options for travelers depending on budget.

Flights:

- Round-trip flights from Los Angeles to Bora Bora can cost between $1,200 to $2,500 depending on the time of year and how far in advance you book.
- Connecting flights from Tahiti to Bora Bora typically cost $150 to $300 for a round-trip ticket.

Accommodation: Bora Bora is home to some of the world's most luxurious resorts, particularly those offering overwater bungalows. However, there are also more affordable options:

- **Budget hotels and guesthouses:** $150 to $250 per night.
- **Mid-range hotels and beachfront bungalows:** $300 to $500 per night.
- **Luxury resorts (including overwater bungalows):** $700 to $1,500+ per night. Premium suites and exclusive resorts can go beyond $2,000 per night.

Food and Dining:

- Casual dining and local eateries: $15 to $30 per meal.
- **Mid-range restaurants:** $35 to $60 per meal.
- **Fine dining or resort restaurants:** $60+ per person.
- The cost of dining is higher at the luxury resorts, where meals at gourmet restaurants can be much more expensive.

Activities:

- **Lagoon tours and snorkeling:** $50 to $150 per person.
- **Shark and ray snorkeling excursions:** $75 to $150.
- **Private boat tours:** $200 to $500+ depending on the length of the tour and inclusivity.
- **Hiking Mount Otemanu:** Free to hike, but guided tours range from $100 to $200.

Transportation:

- Public transport on Bora Bora is limited. Taxis can be quite expensive, with fares around $15 to $30 for short trips.
- Renting a bike or scooter is a more affordable option, costing around $25 to $50 per day.

- Boat rentals for excursions or private tours are also popular but can cost $100+ per hour.

Bora Bora is a destination that lives up to its reputation as a paradise on earth. Whether you're indulging in luxury, seeking adventure, or simply soaking in the natural beauty, Bora Bora offers an unforgettable experience. The island's beauty, charm, and sense of exclusivity make it an ideal place for a romantic getaway, honeymoon, or even just a relaxing escape into nature. While it can be an expensive destination, the memories and unique experiences you'll gain from visiting will make it all worthwhile.

Moorea

Moorea: The Island of Wonders

Located just 17 miles (28 kilometers) from Tahiti, Moorea is often referred to as the "sister island" of Tahiti. Moorea is smaller, more laid-back, and has a distinctly different vibe from its famous neighbor, offering a more tranquil atmosphere and breathtaking landscapes. With its lush mountains, sparkling lagoons, and pristine beaches, Moorea is a place where visitors can truly immerse themselves in the beauty of French Polynesia, away from the hustle and bustle of more tourist-heavy destinations.

What to Explore in Moorea

Cook's Bay and Opunohu Bay Moorea is home to two stunning, crescent-shaped bays—Cook's Bay and Opunohu Bay—both of which offer incredible views, calm waters, and opportunities for exploration. Cook's Bay, named after the famous explorer Captain James Cook, is the more developed of the two, offering plenty of restaurants, resorts, and access to water activities like kayaking and paddleboarding. Opunohu Bay, on the other hand, is more secluded and is known for its peaceful beauty and spectacular backdrop of towering volcanic peaks.
Mount Rotui For an unforgettable panoramic view of Moorea, a hike up Mount Rotui is a must. At 899 meters (2,946 feet) high, it's one of the island's most prominent peaks and offers views of both Cook's Bay and Opunohu Bay. The hike is challenging but well worth the effort, as it provides an opportunity to see Moorea's lush valleys, ridgelines, and crystal-clear waters from above.

Moorea Lagoon Moorea's lagoon is one of the island's most precious natural resources, filled with vibrant coral gardens, tropical fish, rays, and sharks. One of the best ways to experience the lagoon is by going on a snorkeling or diving tour, which will take you to some of the best underwater spots, including Coral Gardens and Le Motu. You can also try a shark and ray feeding excursion, where you'll have the chance to swim with friendly blacktip sharks and rays in the lagoon's shallow waters.
Belvedere Lookout The Belvedere Lookout is one of the most popular viewpoints on the island, offering breathtaking views of both Cook's Bay and Opunohu Bay, as well as the surrounding mountains and lush valleys. It's accessible by a short drive or hike and provides one of the best photo opportunities on Moorea. The area also has a small picnic spot where you can relax and enjoy the scenery.

The Tiki Village Cultural Center If you're interested in learning about Moorea's indigenous Polynesian culture, a visit to the Tiki Village Cultural Center is highly recommended. Located in the heart of the island, this open-air cultural park offers visitors the chance to experience traditional Polynesian dance, crafts, and food. You can watch a Polynesian dance performance, learn about traditional tattooing, and even participate in a famous Polynesian feast (known as a "ma'a tahiti") where fish, meats, and vegetables are cooked in an underground oven.

Mo'orea
Picturesque island with lavish resorts

Moorea

Scan the QR code

1. Open Camera: Launch your smartphone's camera app.
2. Position QR Code: Place the QR code within the camera's viewfinder.
3. Hold Steady: Keep the device steady for the camera to focus.
4. Wait for Scan: Wait for the code to be recognized.
5. Tap Notification: Follow the prompt to access the content.

Moorea's Beaches Moorea offers some beautiful and quieter beaches compared to more tourist-heavy destinations. Temae Beach, with its fine white sand and shallow lagoon, is one of the best for swimming and relaxing. Afareaitu Beach, located near the village of Afareaitu, is another peaceful spot that is often less crowded and offers stunning views of the island's mountains. These beaches are perfect for a day of lounging, swimming, or picnicking.

How to Get to Moorea

- **By Air**: Moorea is easily accessible from Tahiti, where the main international airport is located. Moorea Airport (MOZ), located on the island's northwestern tip, has regular flights from Faa'a International Airport (PPT) in Tahiti. Flights between Tahiti and Moorea are operated by Air Tahiti, and the journey is just a short 15-minute flight. The flight is inexpensive, typically costing $40 to $70 one way.
- **By Ferry**: Ferries are another popular way to get from Tahiti to Moorea. The ferry ride takes about 30-40 minutes, and multiple departures are available each day from the Port of Papeete in Tahiti to Vaiare on Moorea. Ferry tickets cost around $15 to $25 per person, and the ferry ride offers scenic views of the surrounding ocean and islands.
- **By Boat**: Private boats and chartered yachts are also available for those who prefer a more luxurious or personalized journey. These services can be more expensive but provide the option to explore Moorea at your own pace and enjoy its surrounding waters in privacy.

Cost of Visiting Moorea

Moorea is generally considered a more affordable destination compared to Bora Bora, though it still caters to those looking for luxury experiences. Visitors can find a range of accommodation options, dining choices, and activities to suit different budgets.

Flights:

- Round-trip flights from Tahiti to Moorea generally cost between $40 and $70 one way, making it an affordable destination for those already in Tahiti.
- Flights from international destinations like Los Angeles (LAX) to Tahiti (PPT) typically range from $600 to $1,200, with a connecting flight to Moorea.

Accommodation: Moorea offers a variety of accommodation options, from budget-friendly guesthouses to high-end resorts:

- **Budget accommodations and guesthouses**: $80 to $150 per night.
- **Mid-range hotels and beachside bungalows**: $150 to $300 per night.
- **Luxury resorts (including overwater bungalows)**: $300 to $700+ per night, depending on the season and the level of luxury.

Food and Dining:

- **Casual dining and local restaurants**: $10 to $25 per meal.
- **Mid-range restaurants and hotel dining**: $25 to $50 per meal.
- Fine dining and resort restaurants: $50+ per person.
- Many resorts offer all-inclusive packages, which can be a good deal for those staying in luxury accommodations.

Activities:

- **Snorkeling, boat tours, and lagoon cruises:** $50 to $100 per person.
- Shark and ray snorkeling excursions: $60 to $150 per person.
- **Hiking tours (to places like Belvedere Lookout or Mount Rotui):** $50 to $150 depending on the length and guide.
- **Cultural performances and traditional feasts**: $40 to $100 per person.

Transportation:

- **Renting a car or scooter**: $40 to $60 per day.
- Taxis on Moorea are available but can be pricey, with fares starting at $15 to $20 for short rides.
- Rental bikes are a great way to get around the island and are usually available for $15 to $30 per day.

Moorea is a must-visit for those who want to experience the natural beauty and cultural richness of French Polynesia in a more tranquil and laid-back setting. While Bora Bora is famous for its overwater bungalows and luxurious resorts, Moorea offers a quieter escape with just as much beauty, adventure, and charm. Whether you're hiking through volcanic peaks, swimming in crystal-clear lagoons, or immersing yourself in Polynesian culture, Moorea offers an unforgettable experience. With its relatively affordable options for accommodation, dining, and activities, Moorea is the perfect destination for travelers looking for both adventure and relaxation.

Raiatea & Huahine

Raiatea & Huahine: Hidden Gems of French Polynesia

Raiatea and Huahine are two of French Polynesia's lesser-known but equally captivating islands, offering an authentic glimpse into Polynesian culture and natural beauty. These islands are more serene and tranquil compared to Bora Bora and Moorea, making them perfect for those seeking a more peaceful and immersive escape. Both Raiatea and Huahine boast stunning landscapes, rich cultural history, and unparalleled opportunities for exploration.

Raiatea: The Sacred Island

Raiatea, often called the "sacred island," is steeped in history and is considered the spiritual heart of the Polynesian islands. Known for its lush mountains, beautiful lagoons, and ancient cultural significance, Raiatea is the second-largest island in French Polynesia and an essential place for those looking to explore Polynesian traditions and natural beauty.

What to Explore in Raiatea

Mount Tapioi Mount Tapioi, one of Raiatea's highest peaks, offers breathtaking panoramic views of the island's coastline and nearby islands. Hiking to the summit rewards you with an exceptional perspective of Raiatea's lush landscape and crystal-clear waters. It's a moderately challenging trek but worth every step for the mesmerizing view.

The Sacred Marae of Taputapuātea Raiatea is home to the ancient marae (temple) of Taputapuātea, one of the most sacred archaeological sites in Polynesia. The marae is a UNESCO World Heritage site and was once a place of worship and political gathering. It is believed that many Polynesian islands were once united under the sacred rituals performed here. Visiting the site offers deep insight into the spiritual and cultural practices of the Polynesians.

Huahine-Iti
Lush tropical Polynesian island

Raiatea & Huahine

Scan the QR code

1. Open Camera: Launch your smartphone's camera app.
2. Position QR Code: Place the QR code within the camera's viewfinder.
3. Hold Steady: Keep the device steady for the camera to focus.
4. Wait for Scan: Wait for the code to be recognized.
5. Tap Notification: Follow the prompt to access the content.

Raiatea Lagoon Raiatea's lagoon is an unspoiled paradise for water enthusiasts. The clear, shallow waters are perfect for snorkeling, diving, and paddleboarding. Fare Hape is a popular snorkeling spot, where you can encounter vibrant marine life including tropical fish, rays, and sometimes even sea turtles. You can also take a boat tour to Motu Iriru, a small islet in the lagoon, for a day of relaxing by the sea.

Faaroa River The Faaroa River, Raiatea's only navigable river, is a hidden gem for eco-tourism and adventure seekers. You can take a boat or kayak tour up the river to explore Raiatea's lush interior, surrounded by towering mountains and dense tropical rainforest. This serene journey through the river offers a unique perspective of the island's natural beauty.

Cultural Experiences Raiatea's local culture is rooted deeply in Polynesian traditions. Visitors can learn about traditional weaving, dancing, and tattooing. The island is also known for producing Polynesian crafts, including the famous tifaifai (a traditional quilted textile). Attending a local Polynesian cultural show or dance performance gives visitors a deeper understanding of the island's heritage.

How to Get to Raiatea

- **By Air**: Raiatea is accessible by air via Raiatea Airport (RFP), which is served by domestic flights from Faa'a International Airport (PPT) in Tahiti. The flight duration is approximately 40 minutes, and round-trip tickets generally cost $100 to $200.
- **By Boat**: Raiatea is also accessible by ferry from Tahiti. The journey takes about 4 to 5 hours, and ferry tickets cost around $30 to $60 one way. Ferries from Bora Bora to Raiatea are also available.

Huahine: The Island of the Ancients

Huahine is often referred to as the "Island of the Ancients" because of its historical and archaeological significance. The island is known for its ancient temples, crystal-clear lagoons, and lush valleys. Huahine offers a more authentic and less touristy experience compared to some of the more famous islands in French Polynesia.

What to Explore in Huahine

The Marae of Maeva One of the most important cultural and historical sites on the island, the Marae of Maeva is a series of ancient Polynesian temples that date back to the 9th century. The site offers visitors a glimpse into the spiritual and social life of early Polynesian inhabitants. The ancient ruins are surrounded by lush tropical greenery, creating an atmosphere of mystery and reverence.

Huahine Lagoon Huahine's lagoon is a paradise for water lovers, with crystal-clear water and abundant marine life. Snorkelers and divers can explore the Coral Garden near Fare or head to the nearby Motu (small islets) for a peaceful escape. You may encounter rays, sea turtles, and a variety of tropical fish. For those looking for more adventure, Huahine's lagoon also offers the chance to go shark and ray feeding.

Huahine Nui & Huahine Iti Huahine is made up of two parts: Huahine Nui (the larger island) and Huahine Iti (the smaller island). Exploring the two islands by bike or car is an excellent way to experience the island's hidden beaches, coconut groves, and traditional Polynesian villages. Hiking to the summit of Mount Turi offers magnificent views of both islands, and the surrounding landscape is full of rugged beauty and untouched nature.

The Blue Lagoon Huahine is home to the Blue Lagoon, a stunning natural lagoon known for its vivid turquoise waters and abundant sea life. The lagoon can be explored by boat, where you can see local flora and fauna, including the occasional ray or shark. The Blue Lagoon is a secluded area, perfect for a quiet day of swimming and sunbathing.

Huahine's Vanilla Plantations Huahine is famous for its vanilla plantations, and visiting one offers a unique cultural and culinary experience. The island is home to some of the finest vanilla beans in the world, and you can learn about the entire process of vanilla cultivation, from the flowering of the vanilla orchids to the curing of the beans. You can also sample some delicious locally made vanilla products like ice cream, jams, and perfumes.

How to Get to Huahine

- **By Air**: Huahine Airport (HUH) serves domestic flights from Tahiti and is approximately a 45-minute flight away. Air Tahiti operates regular flights between Tahiti and Huahine, and tickets typically cost around $100 to $200 one way.
- **By Boat**: Ferries between Tahiti and Huahine are available and take about 4 hours. The ferry ride offers scenic views of the surrounding ocean and is an affordable option for those traveling between the islands.

Cost of Visiting Raiatea & Huahine

Both Raiatea and Huahine offer a range of options for travelers on different budgets. The cost of visiting these islands is generally more affordable compared to more tourist-heavy destinations like Bora Bora and Moorea.

Flights:

- Round-trip flights from Tahiti to Raiatea and Tahiti to Huahine typically cost between $100 and $200 one way.

Accommodation:

- **Budget accommodations (guesthouses, pensions)**: $80 to $150 **per night.**
- **Mid-range hotels and bungalows**: $150 to $300 per night.
- **Luxury resorts (limited options on both islands)**: $300 to $600+ per night.

Food and Dining:

- **Casual dining and local eateries**: $10 to $20 per meal.
- **Mid-range restaurants**: $20 to $40 per meal.
- **Fine dining (typically at resorts)**: $40+ per person.

Activities:

- **Lagoon tours and snorkeling**: $50 to $100 per person.
- **Shark and ray snorkeling**: $60 to $150 per person.
- **Cultural tours and visits to the marae**: $20 to $50.
- **Vanilla plantation tours**: $20 to $40 per person.

Transportation:

- **Rental cars or scooters**: $40 to $60 per day.
- Taxis and local transport are available but can be expensive, with fares starting at $10 to $20 for short trips.

Raiatea and Huahine may not be as widely known as Bora Bora or Moorea, but they offer an incredible experience for those looking to explore the authentic side of French Polynesia. Raiatea's spiritual and cultural significance, combined with its natural beauty, makes it a must-visit for history and nature enthusiasts. Huahine, with its ancient ruins, tranquil beaches, and rich culture, is perfect for travelers looking to escape the crowds and experience a slower pace of island life. Both islands provide an opportunity to experience French Polynesia at its most serene and authentic, making them perfect destinations for those seeking peace, history, and natural beauty.

Marquesas Islands

Marquesas Islands: The Untamed Beauty of French Polynesia

The Marquesas Islands are the most remote and rugged archipelago in French Polynesia, located about 1,500 kilometers (930 miles) northeast of Tahiti. Known for their dramatic landscapes, rich history, and unique culture, the Marquesas Islands offer a one-of-a-kind travel experience. With jagged peaks, lush valleys, and pristine beaches, these islands provide a true escape from the modern world, making them ideal for adventurous travelers who seek both natural beauty and cultural immersion.

What to Explore in the Marquesas Islands

Hiva Oa: The Land of Paul Gauguin Hiva Oa, the second-largest island in the Marquesas, is famously known as the final resting place of the legendary French artist Paul Gauguin, who lived and worked on the island until his death in 1903. The island offers a blend of historical significance, dramatic landscapes, and cultural heritage.

- **Gauguin's Tomb & Cultural Museum**: Visit Calvaire de Taaoa to see Gauguin's tomb and the Gauguin Cultural Center, where you can learn about his time in the Marquesas and his influence on the art world. The museum showcases some of his works and details about his life on the island.
- **Tiki Statues and Archaeological** Sites: Hiva Oa is home to several ancient Polynesian sites, including impressive tikis (carved stone figures) and marae (sacred ceremonial sites). Notable sites include the Ahu Hapu'u Marae and the Ahu Vai Uri.
- **Hike to Mount Temetiu**: For adventure enthusiasts, hiking Mount Temetiu, the highest peak on Hiva Oa, offers stunning views of the island and the surrounding ocean. The trek through lush forests and steep paths rewards you with breathtaking panoramas.

Nuku Hiva: The Largest and Most Dramatic Island Nuku Hiva, the largest island in the Marquesas, is known for its towering cliffs, vast valleys, and rugged terrain. The island is steeped in Polynesian history and is often described as the "Island of Kings" because it was once the seat of powerful tribal chiefs.

- **Taiohae Bay**: The main entry point to Nuku Hiva, Taiohae Bay, offers picturesque views, and the surrounding village is home to several restaurants, shops, and cultural experiences. Visitors can explore the bay by boat or enjoy the black-sand beaches along its coastline.
- **The Marquesan Ceremonial Sites**: Nuku Hiva is rich in archaeological treasures. The island is home to megalithic sites such as Marae Taputapuātea and the Hatiheu Valley, where you can see ancient tiki statues and explore the remnants of ceremonial grounds.

- **Hiking and Waterfalls**: One of the best ways to explore Nuku Hiva's natural beauty is by hiking to its stunning waterfalls, such as Vaipo Waterfall, one of the tallest waterfalls in the Marquesas. The hike is challenging but well worth it, offering views of lush jungles and jagged cliffs.

Ua Pou: The Island of Peaks Ua Pou is a small but visually striking island, famous for its dramatic, needle-like peaks that rise sharply from the ocean. This island is a haven for nature lovers and offers a chance to experience the Marquesas' wild landscapes up close.

- **The Peaks of Ua Pou**: The island's jagged mountains are its defining feature. These volcanic peaks create a striking landscape that is a hiker's paradise. A guided hike through the island's trails offers incredible views of the steep cliffs, lush valleys, and the ocean beyond.
- **The Village of Hakahau**: The main village on Ua Pou, Hakahau, offers a glimpse into local life with its charming homes and community. The village is also known for its crafts, particularly wood carvings, which visitors can purchase as souvenirs.
- **Traditional Marquesan Culture**: The island's inhabitants maintain traditional customs, and visiting Ua Pou offers an opportunity to learn about the island's distinct Marquesan culture, including its dance, music, and craft.

Fatu Hiva: The Remote Paradise Fatu Hiva, the southernmost island in the Marquesas, is the least developed and most isolated, making it the perfect destination for those seeking complete tranquility and natural beauty. It is an island of lush forests, steep cliffs, and picturesque beaches.

- **Hike to the Bay of Virgins**: One of the island's most famous features is the Bay of Virgins (Baie des Vierges), which is surrounded by dramatic cliffs that create a stunning backdrop. The hike to the bay takes you through dense tropical jungle and rewards you with panoramic views of the bay and surrounding coastline.
- **Traditional Marquesan Art**: Fatu Hiva is known for its traditional Marquesan crafts, including weaving and wood carvings. The island's artisans create intricate jewelry, masks, and sculptures that reflect the island's cultural heritage.
- **Wildlife and Flora**: Fatu Hiva's isolated nature makes it a haven for unique wildlife and plant species. The island is also a prime spot for birdwatching, particularly the Hiva Oa petrel.

How to Get to the Marquesas Islands

The Marquesas Islands are quite remote, and getting there requires a bit of planning. There are no direct international flights, so travelers must first fly to Tahiti and then take a domestic flight.

By Air:

- Air Tahiti offers regular flights to the Marquesas Islands from Faa'a International Airport (PPT) in Tahiti. The most commonly visited islands (Nuku Hiva, Hiva Oa) are accessible by air, with flight durations ranging from 3 to 4 hours.
- Flights to the Marquesas can be pricey, with one-way tickets costing $300 to $500 depending on the island. Flights to more remote islands like Fatu Hiva and Ua Pou may be limited, so it's important to plan ahead.

MARQUESAS
ISLANDS

Marquesas Islands

Scan the QR code

1. Open Camera: Launch your smartphone's camera app.
2. Position QR Code: Place the QR code within the camera's viewfinder.
3. Hold Steady: Keep the device steady for the camera to focus.
4. Wait for Scan: Wait for the code to be recognized.
5. Tap Notification: Follow the prompt to access the content.

By Sea:

- Cargo ships and occasional cruise ships also visit the Marquesas Islands, although travel by sea can take several days. Cruises offer a leisurely way to visit multiple islands in the archipelago, but schedules can be irregular.

Cost of Visiting the Marquesas Islands

Visiting the Marquesas Islands can be more expensive than other parts of French Polynesia due to their remote location and limited infrastructure. However, the unique experience and natural beauty make it worthwhile for many travelers.

Flights:

- Round-trip flights from Tahiti to the Marquesas typically cost between $300 and $500 per person.
- Domestic flights between the islands of the Marquesas (e.g., from Nuku Hiva to Hiva Oa) are generally $100 to $200 each way.

Accommodation:

- Guesthouses and pensions (small, family-run accommodations): $50 to $100 per night.
- Mid-range hotels and eco-lodges: $100 to $200 per night.
- Luxury resorts are rare, but some islands may offer more upscale options, with prices ranging from $200 to $400+ per night.

Food and Dining:

- **Local eateries and casual dining**: $10 to $20 per meal.
- Mid-range restaurants: $20 to $40 per meal.
- Fine dining (limited options): $40+ per person.

Activities:

- Lagoon tours, hikes, and cultural experiences: $50 to $100 per activity.
- Boat rentals and diving: $100 to $150 per person for a day trip.

Transportation:

- Car and scooter rentals are available on larger islands: $40 to $60 per day.
- Local taxis and boat tours are available but can be more expensive due to the islands' remote nature.

The Marquesas Islands offer a unique and untouched side of French Polynesia. With their rugged landscapes, ancient culture, and remote nature, they provide an unforgettable experience for travelers who crave adventure, history, and pristine natural beauty. While the islands can be more challenging to access and may come with a higher price tag, the reward is a serene and authentic Polynesian escape that few have had the privilege to experience. Whether exploring ancient ruins, hiking dramatic peaks, or immersing yourself in the local culture, the Marquesas will leave you with lasting memories of an unspoiled paradise.

Chapter 3. Beaches and Natural Wonders

Iconic Beaches

Matira Beach (Bora Bora)

What to Expect:
Matira Beach is arguably Bora Bora's most famous beach, known for its soft white sand and crystal-clear turquoise waters. The shallow lagoon and gentle waves make it a perfect spot for swimming, snorkeling, and relaxing in the sun. The palm trees that line the shore provide plenty of shade, making it a great place to spend the day. The beach offers spectacular views of Mount Otemanu, Bora Bora's highest peak, and the surrounding coral reefs. Whether you're lounging on the beach, taking a dip in the warm water, or enjoying the vibrant sunset, Matira Beach is a picture-perfect location.

How to Get There:
Matira Beach is located on the southern tip of Bora Bora Island, easily accessible by taxi, rental bike, or scooter from the main town, Vaitape. It is around 15 minutes from the main town and a short drive from most luxury resorts on the island. Many hotels and resorts also offer shuttles to the beach for their guests.

Cost:

- Public Access: Free to visit.
- Parking: There is limited free parking available near the beach.

Activities:
- Snorkeling gear rentals: $10–$20 per day.
- Private boat tours: $150–$250 per person.

Temae Beach (Moorea)

What to Expect:
Temae Beach on Moorea is renowned for its pristine beauty, white sandy shores, and peaceful atmosphere. This beach is a great place to enjoy water activities such as snorkeling, swimming, or stand-up paddleboarding, with calm, shallow waters perfect for beginners. The beach offers stunning views of the Opunohu Bay and the majestic Mount Rotui in the background. It is also less crowded compared to other beaches, providing a more serene and secluded experience.

How to Get There:
Temae Beach is located on the northern coast of Moorea, a short distance from the island's main airport. The beach is accessible by taxi, rental car, or scooter from the airport or nearby hotels, and it's just 5 minutes from Papetoai Village.

Cost:

- Public Access: Free to visit.
- Parking: Free parking available near the beach.

Activities:
- Snorkeling gear rentals: $10–$20 per day.

- Stand-up paddleboarding rentals: $15–$25 per hour.

Haapiti Beach (Moorea)

What to Expect:
Haapiti Beach is a hidden gem on Moorea, offering a tranquil escape with clear, shallow waters and a lush, tropical backdrop. It is an excellent spot for snorkeling, with an abundance of marine life including colorful fish, rays, and sea turtles. The beach is surrounded by coconut trees and offers peaceful, uncrowded shores, making it a perfect place for those seeking relaxation and privacy. Visitors can also enjoy kayaking or paddleboarding in the calm lagoon.

How to Get There:
Located on the west coast of Moorea, Haapiti Beach is about a 30-minute drive from Papetoai Village or Moorea's main town, Maharepa. The beach is accessible by rental car, taxi, or scooter, and it's a popular spot for visitors staying at resorts or vacation homes in the area.

Cost:

- **Public Access**: Free to visit.
- **Parking**: Free parking available near the beach.

Activities:
- **Snorkeling gear rentals**: $10–$20 per day.
- **Kayak rentals**: $15–$30 per hour.

Poe Beach (Tahiti)

What to Expect:
Poe Beach, located on Tahiti's northern coast, is known for its dramatic black sand and vibrant waters, creating a stunning contrast to the lush green landscape. This beach offers great opportunities for surfing, especially during the winter months when the waves are more powerful. It is also a great place for beachcombing, picnicking, or just relaxing by the shore. The surrounding area is less developed, giving it a more rustic and untouched feel compared to other beaches in Tahiti. The beach's volcanic sand makes for an unusual yet beautiful landscape.

How to Get There:
Poe Beach is located about 25 kilometers (15 miles) from Papeete, the capital city of Tahiti. Visitors can easily reach it by car or taxi, with a 30–40-minute drive from the city. It is accessible via the Route des Plages (Beach Road), which offers scenic views along the way.

Cost:

- Public Access: Free to visit.
- Parking: Free parking is available near the beach.

Activities:
- Surfboard rentals: $30–$50 per day.
- Snorkeling gear rentals: $10–$20 per day.

Coral Reefs and Lagoon Exploration

Overview: The coral reefs and lagoons of Tahiti & French Polynesia are some of the most vibrant and ecologically rich in the world. These natural wonders create an underwater paradise, attracting divers, snorkelers, and marine enthusiasts from around the globe. The archipelago's lagoons are home to diverse marine life, including colorful fish, graceful rays, sea turtles, and even sharks. With crystal-clear waters and an abundance of coral formations, exploring these reefs is a must for anyone visiting this tropical paradise.

What to Expect:

- **Coral Reefs**: The coral reefs in Tahiti & French Polynesia are teeming with life. They are protected areas, rich in biodiversity, and are often home to over 1,000 species of fish and 200 types of coral. Some notable locations to explore these vibrant reefs include Moorea, Bora Bora, and the Marquesas Islands.

   The reefs are usually shallow, with vibrant, multicolored corals forming intricate underwater structures that provide shelter to various marine species. For those with snorkeling gear, the shallow depths make it easy to get up close to the coral and observe the incredible underwater world without the need for advanced diving equipment.

- **Lagoon Exploration**: The lagoons surrounding the islands of Tahiti & French Polynesia are peaceful, shallow bodies of water protected by the surrounding coral reefs. These lagoons create calm, sheltered environments where you can swim, snorkel, or take boat tours to explore the marine life. The lagoons' turquoise waters are perfect for activities like stand-up paddleboarding and kayaking.

   The water clarity in these lagoons is exceptional, often exceeding 100 feet of visibility, making it easy to observe the marine life in its natural habitat. Some of the best lagoon exploration experiences include private boat tours, glass-bottom boat trips, and swimming with stingrays and sharks.

Best Locations for Coral Reef and Lagoon Exploration:

- **Bora Bora**: Known for its turquoise lagoons and incredible coral gardens, Bora Bora is a top destination for reef exploration. The coral reefs here are easily accessible by boat or from shore, and snorkeling in the lagoon offers glimpses of vibrant fish, rays, and even blacktip reef sharks.
- **Moorea**: Moorea's reefs are home to diverse marine life, and the lagoon surrounding the island offers shallow, calm waters perfect for beginners. Popular snorkeling spots include Cook's Bay and Opunohu Bay, where you can encounter a variety of tropical fish, turtles, and even dolphins.
- **Rangiroa (Tuamotu Islands):** Rangiroa, one of the largest atolls in the world, is famous for its intense marine biodiversity. Divers often flock here to explore its famous Tiputa Pass and Avatoru Pass, where they can swim with schools of dolphins, manta rays, and sharks.
- **Tikehau (Tuamotu Islands):** The lagoons of Tikehau are especially famous for their incredible coral formations and vibrant marine life. The area is perfect for diving and snorkeling, offering the chance to swim with a variety of fish and see colorful coral walls and underwater caves.
- **Huahine**: Huahine's reefs are pristine and less crowded, offering an authentic, tranquil experience for those looking to explore the underwater world. You can take boat trips to visit the blue lagoons

and surrounding reefs, where you'll find everything from large schools of fish to delicate coral formations.

How to Get There:

- **Boat Tours:** Many of the coral reefs and lagoons are accessible by boat, and there are numerous tour operators across the islands offering guided boat trips to these locations. You can book half-day or full-day excursions to explore the reef, with some tours offering the opportunity to snorkel or dive.
- **Snorkeling and Diving**: Many of the islands have easily accessible snorkeling spots right from the shore. For deeper exploration, certified dive operators are available throughout the islands, providing diving trips to explore the more remote and deeper parts of the lagoon and reef.
- **Lagoon Exploration by Kayak or Paddleboard**: For a more peaceful exploration, renting a kayak or stand-up paddleboard is a fantastic way to venture through the lagoon at your own pace. Most resorts offer equipment rentals for these activities, making it easy to explore the calmer waters near the shore.

Cost:

Snorkeling Gear Rentals: $10–$20 per day, depending on the location.

Boat Tours & Lagoon Exploration:
- Group tours: $50–$100 per person for a half-day trip.
- Private tours: $150–$300 per person, depending on the length and exclusivity.

Diving Excursions:
- Introductory dives: $100–$150 per person.
- Certified diving trips: $150–$250 per person.

Best Time to Visit: The best time to visit for coral reef and lagoon exploration is during the dry season (May to October), when the water is clear, and the weather is ideal for water-based activities. However, the weather in French Polynesia is warm year-round, making it a fantastic destination for underwater exploration no matter the time of year.

Waterfalls and Hiking Trails

Faarumai Waterfalls (Tahiti)

What to Expect:
The Faarumai Waterfalls are a stunning trio of waterfalls located on the northern coast of Tahiti. The falls cascade down lush, green cliffs, creating a picturesque scene surrounded by tropical flora. Visitors can enjoy a short hike through the rainforest to reach the falls, where they can swim in the natural pools or relax and take in the beautiful surroundings. The site is peaceful and less touristy compared to other waterfalls, offering a serene atmosphere. The falls are often surrounded by vibrant greenery, making it a perfect spot for nature lovers and photographers.

How to Get There:
The Faarumai Waterfalls are located about 20 kilometers (12 miles) from Papeete, the capital of Tahiti. The most convenient way to reach the waterfalls is by car or taxi. The site is accessible via a short, well-maintained trail that begins near the road, and it takes approximately 30 minutes to walk to the falls from the parking area.

Cost:

- Public Access: Free to visit.
- Parking: Free parking is available near the trailhead.

Guided Tours:
- Guided hiking tours to the waterfalls: $40–$60 per person.
- Swimming and relaxing near the falls: Free.

Vaipahi Waterfall (Tahiti)

What to Expect:
The Vaipahi Waterfall is located in a beautiful garden setting in Tahiti's interior. The waterfall is framed by lush greenery and offers a stunning natural swimming pool at its base. The area is known for its vibrant plant life, including tropical flowers and towering ferns. The trail leading to the waterfall is relatively short and easy to walk, making it accessible for most visitors. The falls are perfect for a refreshing swim or simply enjoying the natural beauty of the surroundings.

How to Get There:
The Vaipahi Waterfall is situated in the Faa'a Valley, around 25 kilometers (15 miles) from Papeete. Visitors can drive to the entrance and follow a short, well-maintained path to the waterfall. It is recommended to rent a car or take a taxi to reach the location, as public transportation options are limited in this area.

Cost:

- **Public Access**: Free to visit.
- **Parking**: Free parking is available at the entrance.

Guided Tours:
- Guided tours of the falls and the surrounding botanical garden: $40–$60 per person.

Afareaitu Waterfall (Moorea)

What to Expect:
The Afareaitu Waterfall is located on the beautiful island of Moorea, known for its stunning landscapes and lush tropical forests. The waterfall flows down a series of cascading tiers, surrounded by vibrant greenery. The hike to the falls takes you through a picturesque forest trail, where you can experience the rich flora and fauna of Moorea. The falls are relatively easy to access, and there's a natural pool at the base of the waterfall where you can take a refreshing dip.

How to Get There:
Afareaitu Waterfall is located on the eastern side of Moorea, approximately 15 kilometers (9 miles) from Maharepa or Cook's Bay. The trailhead can be reached by car, and visitors can park at the entrance to the hike. The trail is well-marked, and the hike to the waterfall takes around 45 minutes to 1 hour depending on your pace.

Cost:

- Public Access: Free to visit.
- Parking: Free parking near the trailhead.

Guided Tours:
- Guided hiking tours to the waterfall: $40–$60 per person.

Vaimahuta Waterfall (Huahine)

What to Expect:
The Vaimahuta Waterfall is one of the most picturesque waterfalls on the island of Huahine. This waterfall is nestled deep in the island's lush jungle, surrounded by towering trees and tropical vegetation. The waterfall flows from a series of cliffs, creating a stunning cascade of water. The surrounding environment is quiet and peaceful, making it a great spot for a nature walk or swim in the cool pools below. The area is often less crowded, offering a more secluded experience for those who seek tranquility.

How to Get There:
The Vaimahuta Waterfall is located on the western coast of Huahine, near the village of Fare. Visitors can access the waterfall via a short hike from the nearby road. The trail to the falls is well-maintained, though the hike can be a bit steep in parts. It takes around 30–45 minutes to reach the waterfall from the parking area, and a guide is recommended if you want to explore the area more thoroughly.

Cost:

- **Public Access**: Free to visit.
- **Parking**: Free parking available near the trailhead.

Guided Tours:
- **Guided tours to the waterfall**: $40–$60 per person.
- **Swimming in the natural pool**: Free.

These waterfalls offer a mix of easy access, scenic beauty, and the chance to experience Tahiti & French Polynesia's lush natural environment. Whether you're looking for a relaxing swim, a peaceful hike, or a chance to immerse yourself in the stunning tropical landscapes, these waterfalls provide unforgettable experiences.

Hiking trails

Mount Aorai Trail (Tahiti)

What to Explore:
The Mount Aorai Trail is one of Tahiti's most challenging yet rewarding hikes. It leads you to the summit of Mount Aorai, the second highest peak on the island, standing at 2,066 meters (6,811 feet). The trail takes you through diverse ecosystems, from lush tropical forests to alpine meadows. Along the way, you'll experience breathtaking views of Tahiti's rugged mountains, valleys, and coastline. The summit offers a panoramic view of Tahiti Nui and Tahiti Iti. Expect a physically demanding hike with some steep and rocky sections, but the views from the top are well worth the effort.

How to Get There:
The trailhead for the Mount Aorai Trail is located near the village of Arue, approximately 30 minutes from Papeete by car. The trail is not marked for easy navigation, so it's highly recommended to either hire a local guide or be prepared with a detailed map or GPS device. The hike to the summit takes about 6–8 hours one-way, depending on your pace, and it requires a reasonable level of fitness.

Cost:

- Public Access: Free.

Guided Tours:
- Guided hiking tours to Mount Aorai: $60–$100 per person.
- Equipment rentals (if needed): $15–$30 per day for hiking poles, etc.

Afareaitu Waterfall Trail (Moorea)

What to Explore:
The Afareaitu Waterfall Trail is a relatively easy hike that takes you to one of Moorea's most stunning waterfalls. The trail leads you through a tropical forest, where you can enjoy the sights and sounds of nature, before arriving at the waterfall, which cascades down a series of rocky steps into a natural pool below. Along the way, you'll see rich vegetation, including native plants and flowers. This is a family-friendly trail with minimal difficulty, making it perfect for casual hikers or those looking to enjoy a beautiful waterfall without too much physical strain.

How to Get There:
The trailhead is located near Afareaitu Village, on the eastern side of Moorea. It's about a 15-minute drive from Maharepa or Cook's Bay. The hike itself takes around 45 minutes to 1 hour, depending on your pace. The trail is well-maintained and easy to follow.

Cost:

- **Public Access**: Free.
- **Parking**: Free parking near the trailhead.

Guided Tours:
- **Guided tours of the waterfall**: $40–$60 per person.

Mount Tohivea Trail (Huahine)

What to Explore:
The Mount Tohivea Trail is the longest and most challenging hike on Huahine, leading to the island's highest point at 1,241 meters (4,072 feet). The trail offers a mix of dense jungle, rocky paths, and scenic ridgelines. At the summit, hikers are rewarded with panoramic views of Huahine's lush valleys, beaches, and the turquoise lagoons surrounding the island. This hike is ideal for adventurous travelers seeking a true wilderness experience in one of French Polynesia's lesser-visited islands. The trek can be difficult at times, with steep ascents and muddy sections, so it's recommended for more experienced hikers.

How to Get There:
The trailhead for Mount Tohivea is located near Fare, the main village on Huahine. It's best to get there by car or taxi from Fare, which takes about 20–30 minutes. The hike itself can take 5–7 hours round-trip, depending on your pace, with a significant elevation gain.

Cost:

- Public Access: Free.

Guided Tours:
- **Guided hikes to Mount Tohivea**: $50–$80 per person.
- **Equipment rentals (if needed)**: $15–$30 per day.

Taraura Waterfall Trail (Raiatea)

What to Explore:
The Taraura Waterfall Trail is a relatively easy hike on Raiatea, taking you to one of the island's most impressive waterfalls. The hike takes you through the lush, dense tropical rainforest, with the sound of the waterfall growing louder as you approach. Upon reaching the falls, you'll be greeted by a beautiful cascade of water flowing into a natural pool below, perfect for a swim. The area is peaceful and not overly crowded, offering a serene escape. The trail also offers an opportunity to explore the local flora and fauna of Raiatea's protected rainforests.

How to Get There:
The trailhead is located near the village of Uturoa, the main town on Raiatea. It's about a 30-minute drive from Uturoa to the trailhead. The hike itself takes around 1.5 to 2 hours each way, making it a great half-day adventure.

Cost:

- **Public Access**: Free.
- **Parking**: Free parking near the trailhead.

Guided Tours:

- **Guided tours to Taraura Waterfall**: $40–$60 per person.
- **Swimming in the natural pool**: Free.

Chapter 4. Top Attractions

Polynesian Cultural Center

Polynesian Cultural Center (Oahu, Hawaii)

What to Explore:
The Polynesian Cultural Center (PCC) on Oahu is an immersive experience that brings the rich heritage of the Polynesian islands to life. Spread over 42 acres, the center is divided into six distinct island villages: Hawaii, Tahiti, Fiji, Samoa, Aotearoa (New Zealand), and Tonga. Each village offers a glimpse into the culture, traditions, and lifestyles of the people from that region, including traditional arts, crafts, performances, and activities.

Visitors can explore:

- **Cultural Demonstrations**: Watch traditional dances, arts, and crafts being made, and even participate in hands-on activities like hula dancing, tattoo art, or coconut husking.
- **Canoe Ride**: Enjoy a scenic canoe ride through the center's canals to experience the beauty of the landscape and see performances from the various Polynesian cultures.
- **Themed Shows and Performances**: Enjoy live performances showcasing the music, dances, and stories from across the Pacific islands. The Hawaiian Luau Show and the Ha: Breath of Life evening show are particularly popular.
- **Historical Exhibits and Museums**: Discover the history of Polynesian migration and cultural exchanges through informative exhibits and artifacts.
- **Hawaiian Luaus and Dining**: Indulge in a traditional Hawaiian feast with cultural performances during a Luau dinner.

How to Get There:
The Polynesian Cultural Center is located in Laie, on the northern coast of Oahu, approximately 35 miles (56 km) from Honolulu. Visitors can reach the center by car (about 1-hour drive from Waikiki) or via organized tours from Honolulu, which often include transportation and entry to the center. There are also public bus services that run from Honolulu to the center, though a car or guided tour is the most convenient option for tourists.

Cost:

General Admission:
- $69.95–$119.95 per person (based on the package chosen).
- Admission includes access to the village exhibits, shows, and cultural activities.

Luau and Dinner Packages:
- $99.95–$189.95 per person (varies depending on the dining experience and show selected).
- Includes the traditional luau dinner, cultural performance, and the evening show, Ha: Breath of Life.

VIP Packages:
- $149.95–$249.95 per person (includes premium seating for shows, all-day access, and exclusive experiences).

Children's Admission:
- Prices for children (ages 4–11) are typically about 50% less than adult tickets.

Note: Prices vary depending on the time of year, special offers, and selected packages. It's advisable to check for discounts or book tickets in advance, especially for evening shows or special events.

Fautaua Waterfall

Bora Bora Lagoon (Bora Bora, French Polynesia)

What to Explore:
The Bora Bora Lagoon is one of the most stunning and pristine lagoons in the world, known for its crystal-clear turquoise waters, vibrant coral reefs, and diverse marine life. It is the heart of the island's natural beauty and offers a range of activities for visitors to explore. Key highlights of the Bora Bora Lagoon include:

- **Snorkeling and Scuba Diving**: Explore the lagoon's vibrant coral reefs, home to colorful fish, rays, and occasionally, sharks. Popular spots for snorkeling and diving include the Coral Gardens and Motu Tapu.
- **Lagoon Tours**: Take a boat tour to discover the lagoon's various motus (small islets), crystal-clear waters, and the rich ecosystem. Some tours also include shark and ray feeding experiences, where visitors can swim alongside blacktip reef sharks and stingrays.
- **Glass-Bottom Boat Tours**: For those who prefer to stay dry, glass-bottom boat tours offer an excellent way to observe the lagoon's underwater life without getting wet.
- **Private Lagoon Experiences**: Many luxury resorts offer private lagoon experiences, such as private picnics on motus, paddleboarding, or kayaking in the serene lagoon waters.
- **Romantic Sunset Cruises**: Enjoy the stunning colors of the Bora Bora sunset while cruising on the lagoon in a traditional outrigger canoe or luxury yacht.

How to Get There:
The Bora Bora Lagoon surrounds the main island of Bora Bora, which is accessible by plane via Bora Bora Airport (Motu Mute Airport). Flights to Bora Bora depart regularly from Papeete, Tahiti, and other islands in French Polynesia. Once on Bora Bora, you can access the lagoon easily from the Vaitape harbor or directly from resorts located along the lagoon's edge. Most resorts offer boat transfers from the airport to the property, as well as lagoon activities directly from their beaches.

Cost:

Lagoon Tours:
- Standard tours typically range from $50–$150 per person, depending on the duration and type of tour.

Snorkeling and Scuba Diving:
- **Snorkeling trips**: around $50–$100 per person.
- **Scuba diving**: generally ranges from $100–$200 per dive, including equipment.

Private Lagoon Experiences:
- **Private boat charters**: typically cost between $300–$600 per hour, depending on the type of boat and services included.
- **Sunset cruises**: around $100–$250 per person, depending on the type of boat and inclusions.

Glass-Bottom Boat Tours:
- Typically priced between $50–$100 per person for a half-day tour.

Note: Prices may vary based on the season, the level of service, and special promotions offered by resorts or tour operators. It is advisable to book activities in advance, especially during peak travel seasons.

Bora Bora Lagoon

Bora Bora Lagoon (Bora Bora, French Polynesia)

What to Explore:
The Bora Bora Lagoon is one of the most stunning and pristine lagoons in the world, known for its crystal-clear turquoise waters, vibrant coral reefs, and diverse marine life. It is the heart of the island's natural beauty and offers a range of activities for visitors to explore. Key highlights of the Bora Bora Lagoon include:

- **Snorkeling and Scuba Diving**: Explore the lagoon's vibrant coral reefs, home to colorful fish, rays, and occasionally, sharks. Popular spots for snorkeling and diving include the Coral Gardens and Motu Tapu.
- **Lagoon Tours**: Take a boat tour to discover the lagoon's various motus (small islets), crystal-clear waters, and the rich ecosystem. Some tours also include shark and ray feeding experiences, where visitors can swim alongside blacktip reef sharks and stingrays.
- **Glass-Bottom Boat Tours**: For those who prefer to stay dry, glass-bottom boat tours offer an excellent way to observe the lagoon's underwater life without getting wet.
- **Private Lagoon Experiences**: Many luxury resorts offer private lagoon experiences, such as private picnics on motus, paddleboarding, or kayaking in the serene lagoon waters.
- **Romantic Sunset Cruises**: Enjoy the stunning colors of the Bora Bora sunset while cruising on the lagoon in a traditional outrigger canoe or luxury yacht.

How to Get There:
The Bora Bora Lagoon surrounds the main island of Bora Bora, which is accessible by plane via Bora Bora Airport (Motu Mute Airport). Flights to Bora Bora depart regularly from Papeete, Tahiti, and other islands in French Polynesia. Once on Bora Bora, you can access the lagoon easily from the Vaitape harbor or directly from resorts located along the lagoon's edge. Most resorts offer boat transfers from the airport to the property, as well as lagoon activities directly from their beaches.

Cost:

Lagoon Tours:
- Standard tours typically range from $50–$150 per person, depending on the duration and type of tour.

Snorkeling and Scuba Diving:
- **Snorkeling trips**: around $50–$100 per person.
- **Scuba diving**: generally ranges from $100–$200 per dive, including equipment.

Private Lagoon Experiences:
- **Private boat charters**: typically cost between $300–$600 per hour, depending on the type of boat and services included.
- **Sunset cruises**: around $100–$250 per person, depending on the type of boat and inclusions.

Glass-Bottom Boat Tours:
  - Typically priced between $50–$100 per person for a half-day tour.

Note: Prices may vary based on the season, the level of service, and special promotions offered by resorts or tour operators. It is advisable to book activities in advance, especially during peak travel seasons.

Black Sand Beaches (Tahiti & French Polynesia)

What to Explore:
Black sand beaches are a striking feature of Tahiti and French Polynesia, formed by volcanic activity that grinds basalt rocks into fine, dark sand. These beaches are not only beautiful but also offer a unique atmosphere compared to the typical white-sand beaches of tropical islands. Some key features of black sand beaches include:

- **Scenic Beauty**: The contrast between the dark sand, lush greenery, and turquoise waters creates breathtaking landscapes.
- **Volcanic Origins**: The sand's black color comes from volcanic minerals, offering insight into the region's geological history.
- **Peaceful Atmosphere**: These beaches tend to be less crowded, offering a more serene and secluded environment for relaxation or contemplation.

Popular Black Sand Beaches:

- Point Venus (Tahiti)
- Papeno'o Beach (Tahiti)
- Hao Island (Tuamotus)

How to Get There:
Most of the black sand beaches in Tahiti and French Polynesia are accessible by car, with a few requiring a short hike or boat ride to reach. They are often located along the coastlines of volcanic islands such as Tahiti, Moorea, and the Tuamotu Archipelago.

Cost:
Access to black sand beaches is typically free, though certain resorts or activities along these beaches may charge for use of their facilities.

Chapter 5. History & Culture

Ancient Polynesian History

Overview:
The ancient Polynesians are known for their remarkable navigation skills, rich cultural traditions, and the spread of their people across the vast Pacific Ocean. The Polynesian islands, including Tahiti, Bora Bora, and others in French Polynesia, are an integral part of this fascinating history. Polynesia's ancient past is deeply rooted in myths, legends, and oral histories that were passed down through generations, shaping the identity of the Polynesian people today.

Key Historical Aspects:

- **Polynesian Navigation**:
  Ancient Polynesians were master navigators who used the stars, ocean currents, and bird patterns to travel thousands of miles across the Pacific, often in double-hulled canoes. They were the first to settle most of the islands in the South Pacific, including those of French Polynesia. This migration, known as the Polynesian Expansion, began around 1,500 BCE and continued for centuries.
- **Cultural and Social Structure**:
  Early Polynesian societies were organized in a hierarchical structure, with chiefs (ariki) at the top, followed by priests, warriors, and commoners. Polynesian society was highly ritualistic, with elaborate ceremonies, dances, and feasts held to honor the gods and mark important events. They also practiced tattooing, carving, and weaving to express their identity and beliefs.
- **Religious Beliefs**:
  Polynesians believed in a pantheon of gods and spirits that governed nature and human affairs. Tahitian religion, for example, was centered around the worship of gods like Tane (god of forests and birds) and Rao (god of war). Sacred sites called marae were used for ceremonies and offerings, many of which still stand today as historical landmarks.
- **Moai and Marae (Sacred Sites):**
  In French Polynesia and other islands, sacred temples and platforms, called marae, were used for rituals and offerings to the gods. Moai statues, notably found on Easter Island, are perhaps the most iconic relics of Polynesian culture, though similar traditions of stone carving and sculpture were practiced across the region.
- **Agricultural and Artistic Achievements**:
  Ancient Polynesians cultivated crops like taro, yams, breadfruit, and coconut, which formed the backbone of their diet. They also developed distinctive forms of art and craftsmanship, including tattoos, wood carvings, and bark cloth production.

Legacy:
Polynesian history and culture have a lasting impact on the modern world, particularly in the realms of navigation, mythology, and art. Today, many of the traditions and languages of ancient Polynesia are still alive, with ongoing efforts to preserve and revitalize Polynesian culture across the islands of the Pacific. The ancient Polynesians' ability to navigate vast distances without modern technology remains one of the most impressive achievements in human history.

Tahitian Traditions and Festivals

Ori Tahiti (Traditional Dance)

When & Where:

- **When**: Ori Tahiti is performed year-round but is particularly featured during festivals like Heiva I Tahiti.
- **Where**: It can be experienced in various locations across Tahiti and French Polynesia, especially in cultural centers and during traditional celebrations.

What to Expect:

- Ori Tahiti is an integral part of Tahitian culture and features vibrant, rhythmic dance movements, especially with the hips and arms. The dance is often accompanied by the traditional to'ere drum and pahu drums, creating a captivating performance that tells stories of Polynesian heritage.
- Performers often wear traditional costumes made of tiare flowers, feathers, and bark cloth.

How to Get There:

- Ori Tahiti performances are commonly held at cultural venues such as The Maison de la Culture in Papeete, Tahiti, or at various resorts that feature cultural evenings.
- For festivals, it's best to plan travel around the Heiva I Tahiti or other cultural events.

Cost:

- The cost of attending Ori Tahiti performances varies by venue and event. Expect to pay around $10–$50 for cultural performances, with higher prices for private events and festivals.

Tatau (Traditional Tattooing)

When & Where:

- **When:** Tatau is a traditional practice that can be experienced year-round in Tahiti and French Polynesia.
- **Where**: Tattoo parlors across Tahiti, particularly in Papeete and Moorea, offer traditional Tahitian tattooing. Some tattoo artists specialize in designs that reflect Polynesian heritage.

What to Expect:

- Tatau tattoos are deeply symbolic and can represent one's connection to family, ancestry, or important life milestones. The tattoos are often intricate, with geometric designs, waves, and motifs from nature.
- The tattooing process is traditionally done by hand using a comb-like tool and ink, though modern techniques may be used in some parlors.

How to Get There:

- Tattoo parlors are located in major towns like Papeete, the capital of Tahiti, and Moorea. Renowned artists may also offer private sessions by appointment.
- It's recommended to research reputable artists and book a session in advance.

Cost:

- Traditional tattooing prices can vary significantly depending on the size and complexity of the design. Expect to pay around $100–$500 or more, depending on the artist and the tattoo's intricacy.

Heiva I Tahiti (July)

When & Where:

- **When**: Heiva I Tahiti is held every July, typically lasting for several weeks.
- **Where**: The main events are held in Papeete, the capital of Tahiti, at the Place To'ata outdoor stadium and the Maison de la Culture.

What to Expect:

- Heiva I Tahiti is a grand celebration of Polynesian culture, showcasing Ori Tahiti (traditional dances), chanting, singing, and sports competitions. It also features performances of traditional drumming, canoe races, and art exhibitions.
- Visitors can expect a vibrant atmosphere filled with local food stalls, traditional costumes, and a strong sense of community pride.

How to Get There:

- Papeete is accessible by plane from Tahiti's Faa'a International Airport. From there, the festival venues are easily reachable by car or public transport within Papeete.

Cost:

- General entry to the festival is typically free, but tickets for special performances or events can range from $20–$50.

Matairea Dance Festival (November)

When & Where:

- **When:** The Matairea Dance Festival is usually held in November.
- **Where**: The festival takes place in Papeete, Tahiti, often in the Maison de la Culture or other cultural venues.

What to Expect:

- The Matairea Dance Festival celebrates traditional Polynesian dance, with various performances from local dancers, including the Ori Tahiti and Hula. Dances are accompanied by live traditional drumming and singing, with participants wearing colorful traditional attire.
- The festival also includes workshops and showcases of Polynesian arts and craftsmanship.

How to Get There:

- As with Heiva, Papeete is easily accessible from Faa'a International Airport. Venues within the city are typically within short driving distances from the airport or the city center.

Cost:

- Tickets for the festival performances are usually in the range of $20–$50 for general admission, with prices varying for special seating or VIP experiences.

Local Arts, Music, and Dance

Overview:
The vibrant cultural traditions of Tahiti and French Polynesia are deeply intertwined with its arts, music, and dance. These art forms play an essential role in preserving the islands' history, expressing daily life, and honoring spiritual beliefs.

Local Arts:

- Tahitian Art is characterized by intricate wood carvings, paintings, and weaving. Artists often draw inspiration from nature, mythological figures, and ancestral symbols.
- Tifaifai, a traditional Polynesian quilt-making craft, is one of the most notable arts, where colorful fabrics are stitched together to create intricate, symmetrical patterns that tell stories of Polynesian heritage.
- Tahitian Carving includes wooden sculptures of gods, animals, and canoes. These carvings are often found at sacred marae or displayed as art pieces in galleries.

Music:

- Traditional Tahitian Music is centered around rhythmic drumming and chanting. Instruments such as the to'ere (drum), pahu (drum), and ukulele are often used in performances.
- Chants and Songs are often used in rituals, festivals, and storytelling, with melodies passed down through generations.
- The influence of French Polynesian folk music can be heard in modern songs, blending traditional instruments with contemporary styles.

Dance:

- Ori Tahiti, the traditional Tahitian dance, is a vital cultural expression performed to the beat of drums. The dance is marked by energetic hip movements, graceful arm gestures, and expressive storytelling.
- The Hula, influenced by both Tahitian and Hawaiian cultures, is often performed during festivals like Heiva I Tahiti and the Matairea Dance Festival, showcasing colorful costumes and dances that narrate myths, legends, and daily life.

Overall Experience:
Visitors to Tahiti and French Polynesia can immerse themselves in these vibrant traditions by attending cultural festivals like Heiva I Tahiti or exploring local markets and galleries showcasing art and crafts. These art forms are integral to the islands' identity, providing a window into the Polynesian way of life, past and present.

Chapter 6. Local Cuisine

Traditional Dishes to Try

Poisson Cru (Raw Fish Salad)

What to Expect:

- Poisson cru is the national dish of Tahiti, consisting of fresh raw fish (usually tuna) marinated in lime juice and mixed with coconut milk, tomatoes, onions, and cucumbers. It's a light, refreshing dish that reflects the island's coastal cuisine.

Where to Get It:

- **Restaurants:** Poisson cru can be found at many local eateries and restaurants across Tahiti and French Polynesia, especially along coastal areas.
- **Markets**: It is also served at local markets and food stalls, often made fresh using locally caught fish.

Cost:

- Expect to pay $10–$20 for a serving at a restaurant, with prices varying depending on the establishment. Street food vendors or markets may offer it for $5–$10.

Fafa (Taro Leaves and Coconut Milk)

What to Expect:

- Fafa is a traditional dish made with taro leaves cooked in coconut milk. It has a rich, creamy texture and is typically served as a side dish or with meats like chicken or pork. The dish is similar to spinach in texture but has a unique, earthy flavor.

Where to Get It:

- Fafa is commonly served at local restaurants in Tahiti, Moorea, and Huahine. It can also be found in family-run eateries and as part of a traditional Ma'a Tahiti feast.

Cost:

- You can find Fafa as part of a meal at restaurants for around $8–$15. If served during a traditional feast or at a buffet, it's often included in the price of the meal.

Ma'a Tahiti (Traditional Tahitian Feast)

What to Expect:

- Ma'a Tahiti refers to a traditional Tahitian feast, often prepared for special occasions. It typically includes a variety of dishes such as Poisson cru, Fafa, Pua'a (roast pig), Uru (breadfruit), and coconut-based dishes. The meal is often cooked in a traditional hima'a (earth oven), which imparts a unique smoky flavor to the food.

Where to Get It:

- **Resorts and Hotels**: Many upscale resorts on islands like Bora Bora, Tahiti, and Moorea offer Ma'a Tahiti as a special dinner experience.
- **Cultural Centers:** Some cultural centers, such as Maison de la Culture in Papeete, offer traditional feasts during special events or performances.

Cost:

- The cost for a Ma'a Tahiti feast can vary widely depending on the venue. Expect to pay around $40–$100 per person for an all-you-can-eat buffet or a special meal at a resort.

Chicken or Pork with Breadfruit

What to Expect:

- A simple yet delicious dish of grilled or roasted chicken or pork, often served with breadfruit (known as uru), a starchy, potato-like fruit. The breadfruit is usually cooked by roasting, boiling, or frying and is an essential part of the Polynesian diet.

Where to Get It:

- **Local Eateries**: You'll find this dish at many local restaurants or food trucks across Tahiti and Moorea.
- **Markets**: Vendors at the Papeete Market or smaller villages also serve breadfruit as part of traditional meals.

Cost:

- Expect to pay around $12–$25 for a chicken or pork dish served with breadfruit at restaurants. Smaller food vendors or markets may offer this dish for around $6–$10.

Dining Recommendations

La Ora Beach Restaurant (Bora Bora)

What to Expect:
La Ora Beach Restaurant is a beachfront dining experience offering a mix of French Polynesian and international cuisine. The restaurant provides stunning views of the lagoon and Mount Otemanu. Expect fresh seafood, grilled meats, and Polynesian specialties like Poisson Cru. The ambiance is relaxed, with tables set right on the beach for a picturesque dining experience.

How to Get There:

- Located on Bora Bora's main island, the restaurant is accessible by car or bicycle from most hotels and resorts.
- If you're staying at a nearby resort, many offer shuttle services to La Ora Beach.

Cost:

- Expect to pay $30–$70 per person for a meal, depending on your choice of appetizers, main courses, and drinks. The price may be higher if you opt for a fine dining experience or seafood platters.

Le Taha'a Island Resort & Spa (Raiatea)

What to Expect:
Le Taha'a Island Resort & Spa offers an upscale dining experience in a luxurious setting with both French and Polynesian dishes. Guests can dine at Le Vanille Restaurant, where the menu features an exquisite combination of local seafood, tropical fruits, and global flavors. The resort is known for its intimate and romantic ambiance, making it ideal for couples and special occasions.

How to Get There:

- The resort is located on Taha'a, an island accessible via boat from Raiatea (the closest major island).
- Private boat transfers are arranged by the resort, with the journey taking about 30 minutes from Raiatea.

Cost:

- Dining here is on the pricier side, with meals typically ranging from $50–$150 per person, depending on your choices. Special tasting menus or wine pairings can increase the price.

Bloody Mary's (Bora Bora)

What to Expect:
One of the most iconic restaurants in Bora Bora, Bloody Mary's is known for its casual, laid-back atmosphere and outdoor seating. The restaurant serves fresh seafood, steaks, and Polynesian dishes, often with a unique twist. It's a popular spot for both locals and tourists, featuring a bar and a large selection of cocktails. The relaxed vibe makes it perfect for enjoying a sunset dinner by the lagoon.

How to Get There:

- Bloody Mary's is located on the main island of Bora Bora and is easily accessible by car or shuttle from most nearby hotels and resorts.
- The restaurant is a short ride from the Vaitape town center.

Cost:

- Expect to pay around $20–$50 per person for a meal, depending on your choice of dish and drink. Prices are moderate, especially for the quality of food and the iconic location.

Le Coco's (Moorea)

What to Expect:
Le Coco's offers an intimate and upscale dining experience with a focus on French Polynesian flavors and international cuisine. Known for its elegant setting and romantic ambiance, it's an ideal spot for couples and special events. The menu emphasizes fresh seafood, grilled meats, and locally sourced ingredients, with beautiful views of Moorea's lagoon. The restaurant's emphasis on quality makes it a must-try for food enthusiasts.

How to Get There:

- Located on the island of Moorea, Le Coco's is easily reachable by car or taxi from most resorts.
- If staying at a nearby resort, some provide shuttle services to the restaurant.

Cost:

- Expect to pay $30–$70 per person, depending on your selection of appetizer, entrée, and dessert. It's on the higher end of the dining spectrum but offers a memorable and high-quality experience.

Chapter 7.Accommodation

Luxury Resorts

Four Seasons Resort Bora Bora – Luxury Resort

What to Expect:
The Four Seasons Resort Bora Bora is a luxurious, overwater bungalow resort set against the stunning backdrop of Bora Bora's crystal-clear waters and Mount Otemanu. Guests can expect top-notch service, exclusive amenities, and exceptional dining options. The resort offers a range of accommodations, including overwater villas with private pools, beachfront bungalows, and stunning lagoon views. Guests can indulge in world-class spa treatments, enjoy water activities like snorkeling, diving, and paddleboarding, and dine at the resort's gourmet restaurants.

How to Get There:

- The resort is located on Bora Bora's main island, and guests typically arrive via Bora Bora Airport (BOB). From there, you will be transferred by a private boat (approximately 15 minutes) directly to the resort.
- Bora Bora Airport is accessible via direct flights from Tahiti (Papeete), which takes about 50 minutes.

Cost:

- Rates for a stay at the Four Seasons Resort Bora Bora generally range from $1,000–$3,500 per night, depending on the season, room type, and availability. Special offers or longer stays may offer reduced rates, but expect to pay a premium for the high-end experience and private bungalows.

Le Taha'a Island Resort & Spa – Luxury Resort

What to Expect:
Le Taha'a Island Resort & Spa offers an intimate luxury experience set on a private motu (small island) in front of the beautiful Taha'a Lagoon. The resort is famous for its overwater villas and beachfront bungalows, all designed with a Polynesian flair. Guests can enjoy fine dining at the Le Vanille Restaurant, spa treatments at the Tama'a Maitai Spa, and a wide range of water sports activities. The atmosphere is serene, and the resort is a popular choice for couples seeking romance or a peaceful escape. You can also enjoy unique cultural experiences, including Tahiti-inspired cooking classes.

How to Get There:

- The resort is located on Taha'a Island, which can be accessed by boat from Raiatea. Private boat transfers to the resort are typically arranged by the property, and the journey takes about 30 minutes.
- To reach Raiatea, you will need to fly from Tahiti (Papeete) to Raiatea Airport (RFP), which takes around 50 minutes. Once in Raiatea, you will be transferred by boat to the resort.

Cost:

- A stay at Le Taha'a Island Resort & Spa typically ranges from $800–$2,500 per night, depending on the room type, season, and promotions. The price can increase during peak travel seasons like holidays, so booking in advance may secure better rates.

Budget Stays

Fare Vai Moana (Moorea) – Budget Stay

What to Expect:
Fare Vai Moana is a charming, budget-friendly guesthouse located on the beautiful island of Moorea. This guesthouse offers a cozy and relaxed atmosphere, making it an excellent choice for travelers seeking affordable accommodations with a taste of local hospitality. The property is surrounded by lush tropical gardens and is just a short walk from the beach. Guests can enjoy basic, comfortable rooms with private bathrooms, and some units come with kitchenettes for a more self-sufficient stay. Though modest, the guesthouse offers easy access to Moorea's beaches, hiking trails, and local attractions. It is a peaceful and laid-back place to unwind.

How to Get There:

- Fare Vai Moana is located on Moorea, which can be reached by a 45-minute ferry ride from Papeete, Tahiti's main city. Ferries depart frequently throughout the day, and guests can take a taxi or shuttle from the ferry terminal to the guesthouse.
- Moorea Airport (MOZ) is also a 10-minute drive away for those flying in.

Cost:

- Rates at Fare Vai Moana are typically around $80–$150 per night, depending on the season and room type. This makes it a great budget-friendly option for travelers who want to experience Moorea without breaking the bank.

Pension Fare Maeva (Tahiti) – Budget Stay

What to Expect:
Pension Fare Maeva is a modest, affordable guesthouse located in the heart of Papeete, Tahiti. This charming pension offers simple yet comfortable rooms in a local-style setting, with the option for both shared and private bathrooms. The guesthouse features a friendly, family-like atmosphere, and the hosts offer insights into local culture and attractions. Guests can enjoy a small garden, relax in the lounge area, and take advantage of the easy access to downtown Papeete, including markets, shops, and restaurants. The pension is perfect for travelers who want to stay in the capital on a budget and experience Tahiti's city life.

How to Get There:

- Pension Fare Maeva is located in Papeete, the capital of Tahiti, and is easily accessible by taxi or shuttle from Faa'a Airport (PPT), which is about a 15-minute drive away.
- It's also conveniently located for those arriving via ferry from Moorea or other nearby islands.

Cost:

- Expect to pay around $50–$100 per night at Pension Fare Maeva, making it one of the more affordable accommodation options in Tahiti. Prices may vary depending on the time of year, room type, and availability.

Eco-Friendly Options

Blue Heaven Island (Bora Bora) – Eco-Friendly Option

What to Expect:
Blue Heaven Island is a unique eco-friendly boutique resort located on a private motu off the coast of Bora Bora. The resort emphasizes sustainability, offering guests a chance to experience a tranquil, nature-filled environment while minimizing their ecological footprint. The accommodations are overwater bungalows and beachfront villas, built with natural materials and designed to blend seamlessly with the surroundings. The resort features solar energy, organic gardens, and waste reduction programs. Guests can enjoy activities like snorkeling, kayaking, and cultural experiences, all while enjoying Bora Bora's stunning lagoon and coral reefs.

How to Get There:

- To reach Blue Heaven Island, take a private boat transfer from Bora Bora's main island (approximately 20–30 minutes). Transfers are arranged directly through the resort.
- You will first need to fly into Bora Bora Airport (BOB), which is accessible from Tahiti.

Cost:

- Staying at Blue Heaven Island typically costs around $400–$800 per night, depending on the season and the type of bungalow or villa chosen. The eco-friendly luxury experience comes at a moderate price, with rates that reflect the private, serene location.

The Brando (Tetiaroa) – Eco-Friendly Option

What to Expect:
The Brando is an exclusive eco-luxury resort located on Tetiaroa, a private island in French Polynesia once owned by Marlon Brando. The resort's commitment to sustainability and conservation is evident in its design, operations, and guest experiences. The Brando is fully carbon neutral, powered by solar energy and coconut oil. Guests stay in villas designed to maximize comfort while minimizing environmental impact. The resort offers world-class dining, a spa, and various eco-conscious activities such as birdwatching, scuba diving, and guided island tours. The natural beauty of Tetiaroa is preserved, with a focus on marine and wildlife conservation.

How to Get There:

- The Brando is located on Tetiaroa, accessible by a 20-minute flight from Tahiti to Tetiaroa's private airstrip.
- Flights are typically arranged through the resort, and guests are greeted by staff upon arrival.

Cost:

- A stay at The Brando is one of the most luxurious and exclusive in French Polynesia, with prices ranging from $3,000–$10,000 per night, depending on the villa type, season, and length of stay. This price includes all meals, activities, and airport transfers, making it a high-end experience for those seeking ultimate privacy and sustainability.

Chapter 8. Things to Do

Adventure Activities: Snorkeling, Diving, Hiking

Snorkeling in Tahiti & French Polynesia

Overview:
Tahiti and French Polynesia are world-renowned for their breathtaking coral reefs and crystal-clear waters, making it one of the best destinations for snorkeling. Whether you're an experienced snorkeler or a beginner, you'll find vibrant marine life, colorful corals, and underwater landscapes that are truly mesmerizing. The warm, calm lagoons are ideal for exploring aquatic ecosystems teeming with tropical fish, rays, and even sea turtles.

Best Snorkeling Spots:

- Bora Bora Lagoon – The turquoise waters of Bora Bora offer unparalleled snorkeling experiences, particularly around the coral gardens and motus (small islands). Expect to see blacktip reef sharks, stingrays, and a rich diversity of fish.
- Moorea – The shallow waters off Temae Beach and near Opunohu Bay are perfect for snorkelers. You can encounter rays, triggerfish, and parrotfish in the vibrant coral gardens.
- Raiatea & Huahine – The lagoons around these islands are relatively less crowded, offering pristine coral reefs and the chance to see a variety of marine life, including hawksbill turtles and moray eels.
- Tetiaroa – The coral gardens around The Brando Resort are stunning, with diverse fish species and crystal-clear waters, ideal for a relaxed snorkeling experience.
- Maupiti – This less touristy island offers some of the most beautiful underwater ecosystems, with a variety of tropical fish and coral to discover.

What to Expect:

- Warm Waters – The water temperature is typically between 26°C and 30°C (79°F and 86°F) year-round, making it comfortable for snorkeling at any time.
- Clear Visibility – The water around French Polynesia is exceptionally clear, offering visibility of up to 30 meters (100 feet) in some locations.
- Marine Life – Expect to see a variety of species, such as clownfish, butterflyfish, angel fish, reef sharks, mantas, rays, and sea turtles. The coral reefs are colorful and full of life, creating a magical underwater experience.

How to Get There:

- **Snorkeling Tours**: Many resorts and local operators offer guided snorkeling tours that take you to the best spots around each island. These tours typically provide equipment and expert guidance, ensuring a safe and enjoyable experience.
- **Self-Guided Snorkeling**: For those who prefer to explore independently, many beaches and motus offer easy access to great snorkeling locations. Look for areas with clear, shallow waters and accessible reefs.

Cost:

- Snorkeling gear rental typically costs around $10–$30 per day.

- Guided snorkeling tours range from $50–$150 per person, depending on the duration, location, and whether the tour includes other activities like boat rides or shark feeding experiences.

Tips:

- Bring your own snorkel gear if you have it, as some rentals may not be available at every location.
- Avoid touching the coral or marine life to preserve the fragile ecosystems.
- Use reef-safe sunscreen to protect both your skin and the environment.

With its pristine reefs and vibrant marine life, snorkeling in Tahiti and French Polynesia is an unforgettable adventure that offers a glimpse into the stunning underwater world of the Pacific.

Diving in Tahiti & French Polynesia

Overview:
Tahiti and French Polynesia are among the world's top destinations for scuba diving, offering a diverse range of underwater experiences. The region is home to pristine coral reefs, clear turquoise waters, and an abundance of marine life, including large pelagics, colorful tropical fish, and ancient shipwrecks. With warm water temperatures year-round and excellent visibility, diving here is an unforgettable adventure. Whether you're a beginner or an advanced diver, the islands offer a variety of dive sites suitable for all levels.

Best Diving Spots:

Bora Bora – Famous for its shark and ray diving, Bora Bora offers exciting dives, particularly at sites like Tapu and Motu Ahuna, where divers can encounter blacktip reef sharks, stingrays, and large schools of tropical fish. The coral gardens and drop-offs also provide breathtaking underwater landscapes.

Moorea – Known for its diverse marine life and stunning coral reefs, Moorea offers excellent diving opportunities, especially around Opunohu Bay and Cook's Bay. Expect to see manta rays, reef sharks, and schools of jacks. There are also some deeper dive sites where you can explore underwater caves and ridges.

Raiatea & Huahine – These islands are known for their untouched dive sites. You can explore drift dives, wrecks, and caves with abundant marine life, including eels, octopuses, and turtles. Huahine is also home to the famous Coral Garden, perfect for colorful fish and corals.

Fakarava – Located in the Tuamotu Archipelago, Fakarava is a UNESCO Biosphere Reserve and one of the most renowned diving spots in French Polynesia. Famous for its pass dives, it offers encounters with schools of barracuda, gray reef sharks, and whale sharks during the right season.

Tetiaroa – Known for its private island charm, diving around Tetiaroa is exceptional. The Brando Resort offers access to pristine reefs with rich biodiversity, where divers can encounter turtles, rays, and an array of tropical fish.

What to Expect:

- Clear Waters – Visibility is excellent, often ranging between 30–50 meters (100–165 feet), providing unparalleled underwater views.

- Warm Temperatures – Water temperatures range from 26°C to 30°C (79°F to 86°F) year-round, making for comfortable diving without the need for thick wetsuits.
- Marine Life – French Polynesia is home to a rich variety of marine life, including mantas, reef sharks, whale sharks (seasonal), dolphins, rays, sea turtles, and exotic fish species. The area also features a number of underwater caves, walls, and wrecks.
- Coral Reefs – The vibrant coral reefs are healthy and home to a vast range of fish species. Expect to see brain corals, table corals, and soft corals in an array of colors.

How to Get There:

- Most dive sites in Tahiti & French Polynesia can be accessed through local dive shops and resorts that offer guided diving tours. These tours include equipment rental, boat transfers, and a guide familiar with the best dive locations.
- Tahiti (Papeete) and Bora Bora are the primary gateways for diving in French Polynesia, with direct flights from Papeete Airport (PPT) to islands like Bora Bora and Moorea.
- Dive boats typically depart from the main island, and transfers to dive sites are often part of the tour package.

Cost:

- Scuba diving tours typically range from $80–$150 per dive, depending on the dive location, duration, and whether it's a guided or unguided tour.
- Dive packages often offer discounts for multiple dives, with packages for 3–5 dives ranging from $200–$600.
- Full-day dive trips with multiple dives may cost $250–$400 per person, which usually includes boat transfers, guide services, and equipment rental.

Tips:

- **Certification**: It's recommended to have at least an Open Water Diver certification to dive in French Polynesia. However, many dive operators offer introductory dives for beginners.
- **Conservation**: Respect the underwater environment. Avoid touching coral or marine life and be mindful of your buoyancy to prevent damage to the fragile ecosystem.
- **Safety**: Ensure you are diving with a reputable operator that follows safety protocols, including pre-dive briefings and emergency support.

Diving in Tahiti and French Polynesia provides an exceptional experience for divers of all levels. The region's crystal-clear waters, diverse marine life, and unspoiled reefs make it a must-visit for anyone passionate about exploring the underwater world.

Mount Aorai Trail (Tahiti)

What to Explore:
The Mount Aorai Trail is the second-highest peak in Tahiti and offers a challenging hike with breathtaking views. The trail takes you through lush tropical forests, steep ridges, and rocky paths. At the summit, hikers are rewarded with panoramic views of Tahiti's coastline, neighboring islands, and the vast expanse of the Pacific Ocean. Along the way, you might encounter unique flora and fauna, including tropical birds and exotic plants. This hike is ideal for experienced trekkers seeking an adventure off the beaten path.

How to Get There:
The trailhead is located near the village of Papeari on the island of Tahiti, about 30 minutes from Papeete by car. It's recommended to rent a vehicle or join a guided tour to access the trailhead, as public transportation is limited.

Cost:

- Free access to the trail.
- Guided tours can range from $80–$150 per person, depending on the package and guide services.

Afareaitu Waterfall Trail (Moorea)

What to Explore:
The Afareaitu Waterfall Trail is one of the most accessible hikes in Moorea, offering stunning views of the island's lush interior. The trail is relatively easy, with a gentle ascent that leads you through dense vegetation to the Afareaitu Waterfalls. You'll pass by several smaller cascades before reaching the main waterfall, where you can swim in the cool, clear water. The hike also offers scenic vistas of Moorea's valleys and mountainous terrain.

How to Get There:
The trailhead is located near the Afareaitu village on Moorea, about a 20-minute drive from the ferry terminal or 10 minutes from Maharepa. It's best to rent a car or scooter to reach the starting point.

Cost:

- Free access to the trail.
- Guided tours typically cost around $40–$80 per person.

Mount Tohivea Trail (Huahine)

What to Explore:
The Mount Tohivea Trail is a moderately challenging hike that takes you to the highest point on Huahine Island. As you ascend through dense rainforests, you'll be surrounded by unique plant species and an incredible diversity of birds. At the summit, you'll be treated to panoramic views of Huahine's valleys, beaches, and the surrounding islands. The trail also passes through ancient Polynesian archaeological sites, adding a historical element to the hike.

How to Get There:
The trailhead is located near the village of Fare on Huahine, and you can easily reach it by car or scooter from the main town. It's about a 20-minute drive from the ferry terminal.

Cost:

- Free access to the trail.
- Guided tours can range from $50–$100 per person, depending on the operator and duration of the hike.

Taraura Waterfall Trail (Raiatea)

What to Explore:
The Taraura Waterfall Trail takes you through the lush rainforest of Raiatea, leading to the spectacular Taraura Waterfall. The hike offers a scenic journey through the island's verdant valleys, with several smaller streams and waterfalls along the way. At the end of the trail, you'll be rewarded with the beautiful Taraura Waterfall, where you can cool off in the natural pool at its base. The area is also rich in wildlife and plant life, providing plenty of opportunities for nature enthusiasts.

How to Get There:
The trailhead is located near the village of Opoa on Raiatea, about 30 minutes from the main town of Uturoa by car. The route is accessible by car or scooter, though guided tours are also available.

Cost:

- Free access to the trail.
- Guided tours typically range from $40–$90 per person, depending on the tour package and duration.

Relaxation: Spas, Beaches, and Lagoon Cruises

Tahiti and French Polynesia are renowned for their idyllic landscapes, making them the ultimate destination for relaxation. Whether you're looking to indulge in luxurious spa treatments, unwind on pristine beaches, or enjoy serene lagoon cruises, the islands offer a perfect blend of relaxation and natural beauty. Here's a comprehensive look at the relaxation experiences you can enjoy in this paradise.

Spas: Indulge in Tranquility

Overview:
French Polynesia is home to some of the most luxurious spas in the world. Many resorts have built their spa facilities to integrate with nature, offering treatments inspired by local traditions and natural ingredients. Visitors can enjoy a range of treatments designed to rejuvenate both the body and mind, from traditional Polynesian massages to facial treatments using local plant-based products.

What to Expect:

- **Traditional Polynesian Treatments**: Many spas in Tahiti and French Polynesia offer signature treatments using local ingredients like monoi oil (a fragrant coconut oil infused with flowers), tiare flowers, and tropical fruits such as papaya and coconut. These products are deeply rooted in Polynesian culture and are known for their nourishing and healing properties.
- **Signature Massages**: From deep tissue to aromatherapy, traditional Polynesian massages using techniques passed down through generations are designed to soothe tired muscles and promote relaxation.
- **Luxury Spa Facilities**: Many spas are located in serene, tropical settings, often by the beach or overlooking the lagoon. The sound of gentle waves and the lush greenery surrounding you enhance the experience of tranquility.

Top Spas:

The Spa at The Brando (Tetiaroa) – Offers luxurious treatments in a stunning, private island setting.

Deep Nature Spa (Bora Bora) – Known for its beautiful overwater treatment rooms and exceptional service.

Vahine Island Spa (Huahine) – A secluded spa that offers relaxing treatments in an intimate environment.

How to Get There:
Most spas are located within high-end resorts, so getting there often involves staying at the resort or booking a day pass for the spa. Transportation from local airports or towns to the resorts can be arranged through the hotel.

Cost:

- Spa treatments range from $50–$300, depending on the type of treatment, duration, and location.
- Packages, which may include multiple treatments, can range from $150–$500.

Beaches: Paradise for Sunbathing and Swimming

Overview:
French Polynesia boasts some of the most stunning beaches in the world. Whether you're looking for white sand beaches, black sand shores, or secluded coves, the islands offer a variety of options to suit your taste. The calm, crystal-clear waters are perfect for swimming, lounging, and enjoying the natural beauty of your surroundings.

What to Expect:

- **White Sand Beaches**: Tahiti and its surrounding islands offer several picture-perfect white sand beaches, often fringed by coconut palms and sheltered lagoons.
- **Black Sand Beaches**: Created by volcanic activity, black sand beaches like those on Tahiti are unique and provide a striking contrast to the lush greenery of the islands.
- **Secluded Coves**: Many of the islands have secluded beaches, perfect for visitors seeking privacy and tranquility. Some beaches are only accessible by boat, adding an extra element of adventure.
- **Lagoon Waters**: The crystal-clear waters of French Polynesia's lagoons are perfect for relaxing swims, snorkeling, and simply soaking up the sun. The water is often warm, making it ideal for floating or enjoying a leisurely swim.

Top Beaches:

Matira Beach (Bora Bora) – Famous for its white sand and clear turquoise waters.

Temae Beach (Moorea) – A peaceful beach with stunning views of Mount Rotui and calm waters.

Haapiti Beach (Moorea) – A quieter beach with excellent snorkeling opportunities.

Poe Beach (Tahiti) – Known for its black sand and beautiful volcanic backdrop.

How to Get There:
Beaches are easily accessible from most resorts on the islands. Public transport and local taxis can take you to beaches on the main islands like Tahiti and Moorea, but some secluded beaches may require a boat ride or a hike.

Cost:

- Beach access is typically free unless it's part of a resort. Some private beaches on resorts may charge access fees or require guests to book a day pass for facilities like loungers and food.

Lagoon Cruises: A Serene Journey

Overview:
Lagoon cruises are a fantastic way to experience the beauty of French Polynesia from the water. These cruises typically offer a chance to explore the region's stunning coral reefs, pristine lagoons, and uninhabited islands. Whether you're looking for a leisurely afternoon cruise or a romantic sunset tour, these cruises are a perfect way to unwind and take in the spectacular scenery.

What to Expect:

- Lagoon Exploration: A lagoon cruise will take you to remote, uninhabited islands, where you can enjoy a quiet day on the beach or snorkel in crystal-clear waters. Many cruises also include stops at coral gardens, shark and ray feeding areas, or traditional Polynesian villages.
- Sunset Cruises: A popular option for couples or anyone seeking a peaceful evening, sunset cruises offer stunning views of the sun setting over the horizon, painting the sky in shades of orange, pink, and purple.
- Private and Group Tours: You can choose between private cruises for a more intimate experience or join a group tour to meet other travelers. Many cruises offer lunch or snacks, and some even have live music to add to the atmosphere.

Top Lagoon Cruises:

Bora Bora Lagoon Tours – Offers private and group lagoon tours, including snorkeling and shark watching.

Moorea Lagoon Cruise – A popular day tour with stops for snorkeling, swimming, and a picnic on a secluded island.

Tetiaroa Lagoon Cruise – Take a boat trip to explore the pristine waters surrounding Tetiaroa, home to the famous Brando Resort.

How to Get There:
Cruise operators usually pick up guests from their hotels or resorts. You can also arrange a pick-up from the airport or other points on the islands, depending on the cruise package. Most cruises last half a day to full day and are arranged through local tour operators or resorts.

Cost:

- Lagoon cruises range from $50 to $150 per person, depending on the duration, route, and inclusions such as lunch or snorkel equipment.
- Private cruises can be more expensive, ranging from $200 to $600 for a personalized experience.

Tahiti and French Polynesia offer an unparalleled combination of luxury spas, pristine beaches, and serene lagoon cruises that are perfect for anyone seeking relaxation. Whether you're indulging in a traditional Polynesian massage, swimming in crystal-clear waters, or cruising along a secluded lagoon, the islands provide the perfect backdrop for rejuvenation and tranquility. With their natural beauty, warm waters, and welcoming atmosphere, Tahiti and French Polynesia are truly paradise for relaxation.

Cultural Experiences: Traditional Craft Workshops, Festivals

Tahiti and French Polynesia are not only famous for their stunning natural beauty but also for their rich and diverse cultural heritage. The islands' traditions, passed down through generations, are an integral part of the Polynesian identity. Visitors to French Polynesia have the opportunity to immerse themselves in this culture through traditional craft workshops and vibrant festivals. Here's a comprehensive look at the cultural experiences you can enjoy in this enchanting region.

Traditional Craft Workshops: Learn the Art of Polynesian Craftsmanship

Overview:
Polynesian culture is deeply rooted in its artisanal traditions, and French Polynesia offers numerous opportunities to learn about and participate in these age-old crafts. From weaving and carving to making traditional Polynesian garments, the islands' craft workshops give visitors the chance to take home a piece of the culture while also supporting local artisans.

What to Expect:

- **Tatau (Traditional Tattooing)**: One of the most iconic cultural traditions in Polynesia is tattooing. Many visitors choose to get a traditional tattoo as a way of honoring Polynesian heritage. Artists use ancient methods involving a mallet and needles to create intricate designs that carry deep cultural significance. Some tattoo parlors offer workshops where you can learn about the symbolism behind the designs and the art of tattooing.
- **Wood Carving**: Polynesian wood carving is an ancient art that can be seen in the forms of masks, tiki statues, and intricate furniture. Workshops are available in several places, where you can try your hand at carving or watch a master craftsman at work.
- **Weaving**: Weaving is another traditional craft passed down through generations. Visitors can participate in basket weaving workshops, where you'll learn how to make baskets, hats, and other items from natural materials like palm fronds and coconut fibers. These materials are sourced locally and have been used for centuries for both practical and ceremonial purposes.
- **Making Pareos (Traditional Clothing)**: The pareo is the traditional attire of the Polynesian people, often worn by both men and women. Visitors can take workshops to learn how to make their own pareos, where they'll be taught how to tie and wear the garment, as well as how to dye fabric using natural dyes.

Where to Experience These Workshops:

Papeete Market (Tahiti) – Offers a variety of local artisans where visitors can observe craftspeople at work and purchase handmade goods.

Polynesian Cultural Center (Moorea) – A cultural center that offers workshops in traditional Polynesian arts like weaving and carving.

Bora Bora – Some resorts and tour operators offer craft workshops in wood carving and traditional tattooing.

How to Get There:
Workshops are often part of cultural tours or are offered directly through local artisans, resorts, or cultural centers. Transportation to these locations is typically available via guided tours or taxis.

Cost:

- Workshops range from $30 to $100 per person depending on the craft and duration. Special experiences like traditional tattooing can be more expensive, ranging from $150 to $500 depending on the design and artist.

Festivals: Celebrating Polynesian Culture and Traditions

Overview:
French Polynesia is home to a vibrant festival scene that celebrates everything from music and dance to traditional arts and rituals. These festivals are excellent opportunities to immerse yourself in the local culture, as they showcase the islands' rich history and lively spirit. Many of these events take place throughout the year, making it easy for visitors to catch a festival no matter when they visit.

What to Expect:

- **Heiva I Tahiti (July):**
  One of the largest and most famous festivals in French Polynesia, Heiva I Tahiti is a month-long celebration that takes place every July. It is a festival that honors the islands' history, traditions, and culture through dance, music, and sports. The highlight of Heiva is the traditional Polynesian dance competitions (Ori Tahiti), where dancers from all over Tahiti and its islands perform in colorful costumes to the rhythm of drums and chants. Visitors can enjoy the festival's festivities, including music performances, singing, and traditional games.

- **Matairea Dance Festival (November):**
  Held in Moorea, the Matairea Dance Festival is a celebration of Polynesian music and dance. It features competitions between groups from different islands who perform traditional dances like the haka and the ori tahiti, as well as showcasing Polynesian songs and instruments such as the ukulele and pahu drums. The festival also includes food stalls where visitors can sample traditional Polynesian cuisine.

- **Tiare Flower Festival (December):**
  The Tiare Flower Festival is a unique celebration that takes place in Tahiti every December. The event honors the island's national flower, the tiare, which holds great cultural significance. Locals wear garlands of these flowers, and festivities include beauty pageants, parades, and performances of traditional songs and dances.

- **The Coconut Festival (April):**
  Held on Raiatea, this festival celebrates the importance of the coconut tree in Polynesian culture. Visitors can enjoy traditional cooking, crafting, and cultural performances, all centered around the uses of the coconut in daily life. There are also coconut husking and coconut water drinking contests.

Where to Experience the Festivals:

- Heiva I Tahiti (Papeete, Tahiti) – The event takes place across various venues, including To'ata Square and local community centers.
- Matairea Dance Festival (Moorea) – Held at various venues on Moorea, including the Cultural Center.
- Tiare Flower Festival (Tahiti) – Celebrated in the streets and cultural centers of Papeete.
- The Coconut Festival (Raiatea) – Held in the central area of Uturoa, Raiatea.

How to Get There:
Festivals are generally accessible by public transport, taxis, or private car rental. If you're staying at a resort, it's often best to book a cultural tour that includes transportation to the event. For larger festivals like Heiva I Tahiti, shuttle services and organized tours are available from major hotels.

Cost:

- Most festivals are free to attend, though some performances or events within the festival may have a fee, typically ranging from $10 to $50.
- Some festivals, like Heiva I Tahiti, offer VIP tickets for reserved seating, which can cost between $50 to $150.

Cultural experiences in Tahiti and French Polynesia offer a profound opportunity to connect with the islands' deep-rooted traditions. Whether you're learning about traditional Polynesian arts through hands-on workshops or immersing yourself in the vibrant celebrations of local festivals, these cultural experiences provide an unforgettable glimpse into the soul of the islands. These events not only help preserve Polynesian heritage but also allow travelers to experience the warmth and hospitality of the Polynesian people.

Chapter 9. Practical Information

Best Time to Visit

Tahiti and French Polynesia are known for their year-round tropical climate, which makes it an attractive destination for travelers throughout the year. However, the best time to visit depends on what kind of experience you're seeking. The islands have two main seasons: high season (dry season) and low season (wet season). Each season offers distinct advantages and drawbacks. Here's a comprehensive guide to help you decide the best time to visit based on weather, costs, and activities.

High Season (May to October)

Pros:

- *Perfect Weather*: The high season corresponds to the dry season in French Polynesia, offering sunny days, less humidity, and cooler temperatures. Average temperatures range from 75°F to 85°F (24°C to 29°C), making it ideal for outdoor activities like snorkeling, hiking, and lagoon cruises.
- **Ideal for Outdoor Activities**: The calm, clear weather creates excellent conditions for water activities such as diving, snorkeling, and boat tours. With lower chances of rain, visibility is at its best for exploring coral reefs and underwater life.
- **Festivals and Events**: The high season also hosts some of the most popular festivals, like the Heiva I Tahiti (July), celebrating Polynesian culture with dance, music, and traditional events.
- **Best for Luxury Travel**: With the influx of tourists, many luxury resorts offer attractive packages, and the amenities and services are at their peak.

Cons:

- **Higher Costs**: Because this is the peak travel season, accommodation prices, flight costs, and tours are typically more expensive. Expect higher hotel rates and crowded resorts, especially around major holidays and festivals.
- **More Crowds**: The high season sees an increase in visitors, so popular tourist spots, beaches, and resorts may feel crowded, especially during the summer months in the Northern Hemisphere.

Ideal For:

- Travelers looking for sunny weather, outdoor adventure, and a lively cultural experience. Perfect for those looking to enjoy the best of French Polynesia's landscapes and events.

Low Season (November to April)

Pros:

- **Lower Costs**: The wet season coincides with the low tourist season, so accommodation prices, flights, and tours are usually significantly cheaper. If you're looking to save money, this is the time to visit.
- **Fewer Crowds**: Since fewer tourists visit during the low season, you'll enjoy more solitude on beaches, hiking trails, and at resorts. It's perfect for travelers who want a quieter, more intimate experience without the hustle and bustle.

- **Lush Landscapes**: The wet season brings rainfall, which helps maintain the lush, green landscape of the islands. The vegetation is at its most vibrant, and the waterfalls are often more impressive due to the increased water flow.

Cons:

- **Rainy Weather**: The low season is also the wet season, with occasional heavy rain and thunderstorms. Rain is more frequent, especially from December to February. While the rain doesn't last all day, it may disrupt outdoor plans, especially those reliant on clear skies, such as lagoon cruises and hiking.
- **Higher Humidity**: With the rain comes increased humidity, which can make outdoor activities less comfortable, particularly in tropical forests or while hiking. The temperature is still warm but can feel hotter due to the moisture in the air.
- **Cyclone Season**: Though rare, there is a risk of tropical storms and cyclones, especially from November to March. It's important to monitor the weather closely if you plan to visit during this time.

Ideal For:

- Budget-conscious travelers and those who prefer a quieter, less commercialized visit. Perfect for nature lovers who want to see the islands in their most verdant state and for travelers seeking to avoid crowds.

Shoulder Season (April & November)

Pros:

- **Balanced Weather:** The shoulder months of April and November offer a sweet spot between the extremes of high and low seasons. Weather during this time is often a mix of sunny days and light showers, providing a balance between the ideal conditions of the high season and the reduced rain of the low season.
- **Moderate Prices**: Accommodation prices are lower than the high season but not as low as during the full wet season. You can take advantage of cheaper rates and still experience good weather.
- **Fewer Tourists**: These months are not as crowded as the peak high season, so you'll experience a more relaxed atmosphere while still enjoying the island's amenities and activities.

Cons:

- **Unpredictable Weather**: Although the weather is generally pleasant, there can still be occasional rainfall, particularly in November. Conditions may not be as predictable as in the dry season.
- **Limited Festivals & Events**: While some cultural festivals may be held in these months, the shoulder season lacks the large-scale celebrations that occur during the high season.

Ideal For:

- Travelers seeking a compromise between good weather, fewer crowds, and lower prices. Great for those who want to enjoy outdoor activities without paying high season prices.

Getting Around the Islands

Getting to Tahiti & French Polynesia by Flight: A Comprehensive Guide

Traveling to Tahiti and French Polynesia by air is relatively straightforward, though the islands' remote location in the South Pacific means that most travelers will need to connect through major international hubs before reaching their final destination. Here's everything you need to know about getting to French Polynesia by flight, including major airports, airlines, connections, and tips for a smooth journey.

Major International Airports in French Polynesia

French Polynesia consists of over 100 islands, but the most important airport for international flights is Fa'a'ā International Airport (PPT), located on Tahiti (the largest island in the archipelago). This is the main gateway for international travelers arriving in the region.

Fa'a'ā International Airport (PPT) - Tahiti:
- This is the main international airport in French Polynesia and the hub for international and inter-island flights. It is located near Pape'ete, the capital of French Polynesia.
- Most international flights to French Polynesia arrive at this airport, and from there, travelers can take domestic flights to other islands such as Bora Bora, Moorea, and Huahine.

Other Airports:
- Moorea Airport (MOZ) and Bora Bora Airport (BOB) are the most frequented domestic airports, typically accessible by short flights from Tahiti. These airports mainly handle flights from the capital island.

Airlines That Fly to Tahiti & French Polynesia

Several international airlines and regional carriers provide direct and connecting flights to Tahiti. Depending on where you are flying from, you may need to connect through major international hubs such as Los Angeles, Auckland, or Paris.

International Airlines Flying to Tahiti

Air Tahiti Nui:
- Air Tahiti Nui is the primary airline of French Polynesia and offers direct flights from major cities like Los Angeles (LAX), Paris (CDG), Auckland (AKL), and Tokyo (NRT).
- It operates daily flights from Los Angeles to Tahiti, making it one of the most convenient options for U.S. travelers.

Air France:
- Air France offers direct flights from Paris (Charles de Gaulle Airport) to Fa'a'ā International Airport.
- This is the best option for travelers coming from Europe.

Hawaiian Airlines:
- Hawaiian Airlines also offers direct flights from Honolulu (HNL) to Tahiti. This can be a good option for travelers already in Hawaii or those coming from the West Coast.

American Airlines:
- American Airlines offers seasonal flights from Los Angeles (LAX) to Pape'ete in partnership with Air Tahiti Nui.
- This is another option for U.S. travelers.

Air New Zealand:

- For travelers from New Zealand, Air New Zealand offers flights to Tahiti from Auckland, either as direct services or with a brief stopover in Auckland.

Regional Airlines and Connections

Air Tahiti:
- Air Tahiti is the local airline that operates domestic flights between Tahiti and other islands within French Polynesia, including Moorea, Bora Bora, Raiatea, Huahine, and more.
- Most international travelers arriving in Tahiti will connect with Air Tahiti to reach their final destination islands.

Flight Duration

The flight duration to Tahiti will vary depending on where you are flying from:

From Los Angeles (LAX) to Tahiti (PPT):
- Approx. 8 hours direct flight.

From Paris (CDG) to Tahiti (PPT):
- Approx. 22 hours (with one stopover, typically in Los Angeles or other hubs).

From Auckland (AKL) to Tahiti (PPT):
- Approx. 5 hours direct flight.

From Honolulu (HNL) to Tahiti (PPT):
- Approx. 6 hours direct flight.

From Tokyo (NRT) to Tahiti (PPT):
- Approx. 11 hours (with a stopover, typically in Auckland).

How to Get from Fa'a'ā International Airport (PPT) to Your Hotel or Resort

Upon arrival at Fa'a'ā International Airport, you have several options to reach your accommodation on Tahiti or any other island in French Polynesia:

Airport Transfers:

- Most resorts and hotels in Tahiti offer airport transfer services. You can book these in advance, and many hotels provide shuttle buses or private cars that pick up guests directly from the airport.

Taxis:

- Taxis are available outside the airport, and rides into Pape'ete (the capital) typically cost around XPF 1,500–2,000 (approximately USD 15–20).
- Taxis to more distant destinations such as resorts on Tahiti's west coast can cost more.

Public Transport:

- Public buses are available, but they may not be the most convenient, especially if you're traveling with luggage.

Domestic Flights to Other Islands:

- If you're planning to visit other islands (e.g., Bora Bora, Moorea, or Huahine), Air Tahiti offers frequent domestic flights from Tahiti. These flights typically last between 30 minutes to 1 hour, depending on your destination.

Costs of Flights to Tahiti & French Polynesia

Round-Trip Flights from the U.S. (Los Angeles to Tahiti):

- Prices typically range from USD 700 to 1,500, depending on the season and booking time.

Round-Trip Flights from Europe (Paris to Tahiti):

- Prices range from EUR 1,000 to 2,000 for a round-trip, depending on the airline and season.

Round-Trip Flights from New Zealand (Auckland to Tahiti):

- Expect to pay around NZD 700 to 1,500.

Round-Trip Flights from Australia (Sydney to Tahiti):

- Prices range from AUD 800 to 1,500.

Note: Prices can fluctuate depending on factors like booking time, seasonal demand, and airline promotions. It's advisable to book early and compare flight deals to get the best prices.

Tips for Booking Flights to Tahiti & French Polynesia

Book in Advance:
- Given the popularity of the islands during the high season, it's highly recommended to book flights several months in advance, especially for travel between May and October.

Look for Package Deals:
- Many travel agencies offer package deals that include flights, accommodation, and excursions. These can provide savings, especially during the shoulder seasons.

Check for Seasonal Offers:
- Airlines and resorts often offer promotions during the low season (November to April). Look out for these deals to save money.

Flexible Dates:
- If your travel dates are flexible, you can take advantage of cheaper flights during the week or outside peak periods.

Getting to Tahiti and French Polynesia by flight is convenient with multiple options for direct and connecting flights from major international hubs. The flight journey may vary in duration, depending on where you're coming from, but it typically ranges from 6 to 22 hours. Upon arrival at Fa'a'ā International Airport, you can easily access airport transfers or domestic flights to your final destination island. By booking in advance and being flexible with travel dates, you can ensure a smooth and cost-effective journey to this paradise in the South Pacific.

Getting to Tahiti & French Polynesia by Ferry:

While flying is the most common way to reach Tahiti and the other islands of French Polynesia, there are also ferry services available within the archipelago for island-hopping and transportation between the islands. Ferries are an excellent way to explore the islands at a more leisurely pace, offering stunning sea views and a more relaxed travel experience. This guide will cover the different ferry options available for traveling within French Polynesia.

Inter-Island Ferries: Connecting the Islands of French Polynesia

French Polynesia is an archipelago made up of over 100 islands, many of which are not served by airports. Ferries are essential for traveling between some of these islands, especially within the Society Islands (where Tahiti, Moorea, Bora Bora, and others are located) and the Tuamotu Archipelago.

Types of Ferries:

- **Passenger Ferries**: These ferries are designed primarily for transporting people and are the most commonly used for travel between the main islands. They typically offer basic facilities and can be a more affordable option than flights.
- **Cargo Ferries**: Some ferries also carry freight, including vehicles, goods, and supplies, but many also allow passengers to travel between the islands.

Ferry Routes:

- **Tahiti to Moorea:**
  One of the most popular ferry routes in French Polynesia is the route between Tahiti (Pape'ete) and Moorea, which is located just 17 kilometers away. The ferry ride offers scenic views of both islands and takes about 30 to 40 minutes. Moorea is a popular destination for day trips from Tahiti, as it offers stunning beaches, hiking trails, and traditional Polynesian culture.

Ferry Operator: Aremiti and Terevau are the two main ferry companies operating this route.
- **Cost**: The cost is generally affordable, with tickets ranging from XPF 1,500 to 2,000 for a one-way adult ticket. For vehicles, it can cost around XPF 5,000 to 7,000 for a car.
- **Departure Points**: The ferries leave from Pape'ete Harbour (Tahiti) and arrive at Vaiare (Moorea).

Tahiti to Huahine, Raiatea, and Tahaa:
Ferries also connect Tahiti to other islands like Huahine, Raiatea, and Tahaa, which are located in the Society Islands. These islands are less frequented by tourists, making them ideal for a more tranquil experience.

- **Ferry Operator**: Terevau and Hawaiki Nui are the primary ferry companies that serve this route.
- **Cost**: The ferry from Tahiti to Raiatea, for example, costs around XPF 3,000 to 5,000 one-way for adults, with additional costs for vehicles.
- **Duration**: The ferry ride to Raiatea takes approximately 3 to 4 hours, depending on the island and the specific route.

Tahiti to Bora Bora:
While Bora Bora is primarily reached by air, there are ferry services from Tahiti to Raiatea, and from Raiatea, you can catch a smaller boat or a transfer to Bora Bora. Ferries from Tahiti to Raiatea offer an opportunity to explore the more remote and peaceful islands before heading to the famous Bora Bora.

- **Cost**: Ferry tickets from Tahiti to Raiatea are approximately XPF 4,500 to 6,000, and from Raiatea to Bora Bora, smaller boats may charge around XPF 1,500 to 3,000 per person.

Other Routes:
Ferries also operate to the Tuamotu Islands, Marquesas Islands, and other lesser-visited regions. However, these routes may be less frequent and take longer due to the distances involved.

Ferry Services for Day Trips and Tours

Ferries are also popular for day trips or organized tours between the islands. These ferries typically provide more comfort and are part of a day tour package that includes guided excursions, snorkeling, and visits to secluded beaches or lagoons.

- **Island-Hopping Tours**: Operators in Tahiti offer ferry-based tours to Moorea, Huahine, and Bora Bora, where you can explore lush landscapes, experience local culture, and enjoy outdoor activities.

- **Lagoon Cruises**: There are several companies that combine ferry rides with lagoon cruises for tourists who wish to explore the turquoise waters of French Polynesia. Some tours offer lunch on board, guided snorkeling, or even visits to nearby motu (small islands) where you can enjoy a pristine beach experience.

Booking and Ferry Schedules

Ferry schedules are typically consistent throughout the year, but they can be affected by weather conditions, particularly during the rainy season (November to April). It is advisable to check schedules and availability in advance, especially if traveling during peak tourist seasons or around local festivals.

- **Booking**: You can book ferry tickets in advance via online platforms or at the ferry terminal. It's often possible to purchase tickets directly from the ferry company at the harbor, but booking ahead is recommended during busy periods.
- **Ferry Departure Times**: Ferries from Tahiti to Moorea run frequently throughout the day, while services to other islands may operate less regularly.

Cost of Ferry Travel

Ferry travel is typically much more affordable than flights, making it an excellent option for island-hopping and exploring the smaller islands in French Polynesia.

- **Tahiti to Moorea**: Around XPF 1,500 to 2,000 one way for passengers, with vehicle fares varying from XPF 5,000 to 7,000.
- **Tahiti to Raiatea**: Between XPF 3,000 to 5,000 for passengers, with extra charges for vehicles.
- **Tahiti to Bora Bora (via Raiatea):** Ferry to Raiatea costs around XPF 4,500 to 6,000, and the boat from Raiatea to Bora Bora costs around XPF 1,500 to 3,000.

Tips for Ferry Travel in French Polynesia

- **Arrive Early**: Ferry terminals can get crowded, especially during peak seasons. Arriving early will give you plenty of time to find parking (if needed) and board your ferry.
- **Bring Essentials**: Pack light, comfortable clothing and carry sunscreen, a hat, and a camera. Some ferries have basic amenities like snacks and drinks, but it's wise to bring your own food and water, especially for longer journeys.
- **Check Weather**: Weather conditions can impact ferry schedules, particularly during storms or rough seas. Always check the forecast before traveling and stay in touch with ferry operators for real-time updates.

While ferry travel is not the primary means of reaching Tahiti or other islands of French Polynesia, it is an essential mode of transportation for getting around the archipelago. Ferries offer a scenic, leisurely way to explore multiple islands and provide access to places not served by air travel. Whether you're hopping between Tahiti and Moorea, or traveling further to more remote destinations like Raiatea, Bora Bora, or Huahine, ferry rides allow you to experience the natural beauty of French Polynesia at a relaxed pace.

Getting Around the Islands

Traveling around the islands of Tahiti and French Polynesia can be an incredible experience, offering both breathtaking views and a chance to explore local culture. While flying and ferries are the primary modes of getting between the islands, once you're on the islands, various transportation options are available. From leisurely strolls on foot to more adventurous bike rides or driving, each mode of transport offers a different experience. This guide provides a detailed look at getting around the islands by foot, car, bicycle, and bus.

Getting Around by Foot

Walking is one of the most pleasant ways to explore the islands, particularly in Tahiti, Moorea, and Bora Bora, where scenic routes, coastal paths, and small towns provide the perfect setting for a leisurely stroll.

What to Expect:

- **Scenic Views**: Many areas, especially in Tahiti and Moorea, are easily accessible on foot. You'll find walking paths along beaches, through villages, and up to popular attractions like Mount Aorai or the Afareaitu Waterfall trail.
- **Accessible Towns**: Pape'ete (Tahiti) and Vaiare (Moorea) are pedestrian-friendly, with shops, cafes, and markets all within walking distance.
- **Cultural Immersion**: Walking allows for deeper engagement with the local culture, giving you the chance to interact with residents and experience the island lifestyle up close.

How to Get Around:

- **Popular Routes**: Explore Pape'ete's markets, walk along Matira Beach (Bora Bora), or take the Afareaitu Waterfall Trail (Moorea).
- **Cost**: Free. However, you may choose to pay for guided walking tours or excursions if you prefer a more structured experience.

Tips:

- Be prepared for tropical heat and bring water and sunscreen.
- Some areas, especially more rural locations, might not have clearly marked sidewalks or paths, so it's important to walk carefully and wear comfortable shoes.

Getting Around by Car

Renting a car is one of the most convenient and flexible ways to explore Tahiti, Moorea, and other islands. Whether you're driving along the coastline, exploring remote beaches, or heading to more rugged terrains, having a car will give you the freedom to explore at your own pace.

What to Expect:

- **Scenic Drives**: The roads around Tahiti and Moorea offer stunning views of the ocean, mountains, and lush landscapes. Popular routes include the Ring Road around Tahiti and the drive to Belvedere Lookout in Moorea.
- **Island Accessibility**: While most major roads are paved and easy to navigate, some roads in more rural or remote areas may be unpaved or bumpy.
- **Size of the Islands**: Tahiti is relatively large, and driving across it can take around 1 to 1.5 hours. On Moorea, the island is small enough to easily drive around in a day.

How to Get Around:

- **Rent a Car**: Rental companies are available in Pape'ete (Tahiti) and Vaiare (Moorea). Cars can be rented directly at airports or local agencies. You will need a valid driver's license, and driving is on the right-hand side.
- **Driving Routes**: Explore the Mount Aorai Trail on Tahiti, take a coastal drive on Moorea, or enjoy the winding roads leading to the Faarumai Waterfalls (Tahiti).
- **Cost**: Car rentals generally range from XPF 6,000 to 10,000 per day for a standard vehicle. For compact cars, expect prices around XPF 5,000 to 8,000 per day.

Tips:

- Roads can be narrow and winding, especially in mountainous areas.
- Watch out for pedestrians, cyclists, and animals on the road.
- Gas stations are available, but refueling options may be limited in more remote areas, so it's best to fill up when you can.

Getting Around by Bicycle

Cycling is a fantastic way to enjoy the natural beauty of Tahiti and Moorea at a more relaxed pace. Many tourists choose to rent bikes for shorter trips or for sightseeing, as it allows for a more immersive experience.

What to Expect:

- **Cycling Paths**: In Tahiti, there are limited designated bike lanes, but it is generally safe to cycle along the coast or in more rural areas. Moorea offers better opportunities for cycling, with peaceful roads and picturesque landscapes.
- **Scenic Routes**: Cycle along the coast, pass by lush valleys, or explore the beaches at your own pace. For a fun day out, rent a bike to cycle to Belvedere Lookout on Moorea, or ride along Temae Beach.
- **Relaxed Pace**: Cycling allows you to stop whenever you want, making it ideal for those who want to take in the sights slowly.

How to Get Around:

- **Rent a Bike**: Many local businesses and resorts on Tahiti and Moorea offer bike rentals, ranging from standard bikes to mountain bikes for more adventurous rides. Rental prices typically range from XPF 1,500 to 3,000 per day.
- **Cycling Routes**: Popular cycling routes include the coastal roads around Moorea, Tahiti's west coast, and the area around Papeari. You can also cycle to Mount Tohivea or along the Faa'a road in Tahiti.

Cost:

- Standard bike rentals are typically around XPF 1,500 to 2,500 per day. More specialized bikes, like mountain bikes or electric bikes, may cost slightly more.

Tips:

- Always wear a helmet (most rentals provide them).
- Bring plenty of water, as cycling in the tropical heat can be strenuous.
- Be aware of road traffic and, in some areas, unpaved roads that may not be suitable for all types of bikes.

Getting Around by Bus

The bus system in Tahiti and Moorea provides an affordable and convenient way to travel around the islands, especially for those staying in urban areas like Pape'ete and Vaiare. The bus network connects major towns and tourist areas, making it easy to explore without the need for a rental car.

What to Expect:

- **Public Buses**: In Tahiti, buses are the most common form of public transport. They travel along the coast and connect key towns, resorts, and attractions. Moorea has a limited bus service that primarily runs between the ferry terminal and major tourist spots.
- **Cost-Effective**: Buses are cheap, with fares starting around XPF 150 to 300 for one-way travel, depending on the route.
- **Limited Schedules**: Bus schedules can be irregular, and the frequency may decrease in the evening or on weekends.

How to Get Around:

- **Public Buses in Tahiti**: Buses run frequently from Pape'ete to towns like Faaa, Papeari, and Arue. Routes may also serve major attractions like the Faarumai Waterfalls or the Museum of Tahiti.
- **Moorea Buses**: On Moorea, buses run from Vaiare Port to various resorts, beaches, and local attractions.

Cost:

- The typical fare for a bus ride in Tahiti is XPF 150 to 300. For Moorea, bus fares are around XPF 300 to 600.

Tips:

- Bus schedules may not be as regular or reliable as private transport, so plan accordingly.
- Carry cash, as buses typically don't accept cards.
- Buses may not reach more remote spots, so consider a taxi or rental car for further exploration.

Getting around Tahiti and French Polynesia offers a variety of options to suit every type of traveler. Whether you enjoy the freedom of driving, the slow-paced exploration on foot, the adventurous spirit of cycling, or the affordable option of bus transport, each mode of transportation has its advantages.

- Walking is ideal for exploring small towns and beaches at a leisurely pace.
- Renting a car provides the flexibility to explore at your own speed, especially for those looking to visit more remote locations.
- Cycling offers a wonderful way to immerse yourself in the environment, especially on Moorea.
- Buses are budget-friendly and practical for getting around the main islands, though their schedules may not always be convenient for travelers with tight itineraries.

Ultimately, how you get around depends on your preferences, budget, and the type of experience you want during your visit to these beautiful islands.

Safety and Health Tips

Traveling to Tahiti and French Polynesia is a dream for many, thanks to the stunning landscapes, pristine beaches, and rich cultural heritage. However, as with any international destination, it's essential to stay informed and prepared for the unique health and safety considerations of these islands. Here's a comprehensive guide to ensure your trip remains safe and enjoyable.

Health Precautions

Vaccinations:

- **Recommended Vaccinations**: While there are no specific vaccines required to travel to French Polynesia, it's always a good idea to be up to date on routine vaccinations such as measles, mumps, rubella (MMR), tetanus, and diphtheria. Hepatitis A and B vaccinations are also recommended, as well as Typhoid if you plan to visit more rural or less developed areas.
- **Travel Insurance**: Ensure you have comprehensive travel insurance that covers any potential medical expenses, including evacuation if necessary.

Water & Food Safety:

Drinking Water: In urban areas like Pape'ete (Tahiti), the tap water is generally safe to drink. However, in more rural areas, it's safer to stick to bottled water. If in doubt, opt for bottled water throughout your trip.
- **Food Hygiene**: Street food is part of the local culture, but always check that food is prepared fresh and served hot. Avoid consuming raw or undercooked seafood if you're unsure about its freshness.
- **Poisson Cru (Raw Fish Salad):** One of the region's traditional dishes, while delicious, should be consumed with caution if you have a sensitive stomach.

Mosquito-Borne Diseases:

Dengue Fever and Zika Virus: These diseases are present in tropical regions, including French Polynesia, especially in warmer months. Protect yourself from mosquito bites by:
- Using DEET-based insect repellents.
- Wearing long sleeves and pants in the early morning or evening.
- Sleeping under mosquito nets when possible, especially in rural accommodations.

Sun Protection:

The sun in Tahiti and French Polynesia is intense, so take precautions:
- Apply a broad-spectrum sunscreen (SPF 30 or higher) frequently, especially after swimming.
- Wear hats, sunglasses, and light, breathable clothing to minimize sun exposure.
- Seek shade, particularly between 10 AM and 4 PM, when the sun is at its peak.

Safety Considerations

Swimming and Water Safety:

- **Strong Currents:** Some beaches in Tahiti and Moorea have strong rip currents, especially near public beaches or surf spots. Always swim in designated areas, and heed any posted warning signs.
- **Sharks:** While sharks are present in the waters of French Polynesia, attacks are extremely rare. It's advisable to avoid swimming alone, especially in deep waters, and to stay away from areas where there's an active fishing industry.
- **Jellyfish:** There are some species of jellyfish in the waters, particularly during the warmer months (November to April). Always check with locals about water conditions before swimming.

Beach Safety:

- Some beaches, like Matira Beach (Bora Bora), are shallow and ideal for families. However, always check the water conditions before swimming, especially after storms.
- Sunburn and Dehydration: Avoid spending too much time under the direct sun without protection. Drink plenty of water throughout the day to stay hydrated, particularly if you're out exploring or participating in outdoor activities.

Wildlife and Flora:

- **Poisonous Plants:** Some plants in French Polynesia may cause skin irritation. Always wear gloves or long sleeves when handling plants.
- **Animals:** Dogs and other animals are generally safe, but it's wise to avoid unfamiliar animals to prevent potential bites or scratches.

Emergency Contacts and Services

Emergency Numbers:

- Police: 17
- Ambulance: 18
- Fire Department: 18
- General Emergency Line (Tahiti and Moorea): 112

Medical Services:

- **Pape'ete Hospital (Tahiti):** The Hospital of Tahiti is the largest medical facility and can handle most emergency situations. Smaller clinics exist in other towns but may not have the same resources.
- **Pharmacies:** Pharmacies are available on most islands. Pape'ete and Moorea have well-stocked pharmacies, while more remote islands may have limited supplies. It's always a good idea to carry

basic medication, including pain relievers, antihistamines, and anything prescribed for chronic conditions.

Safety Tips for Exploring the Islands

Traveling in Remote Areas:

- If you plan to venture into more isolated areas like the Marquesas Islands or Raiatea, let someone know your itinerary and estimated return time.
- Consider joining a guided tour if you are unfamiliar with the area, especially for activities like hiking or exploring remote beaches.

Driving Safety:

- While driving in Tahiti and Moorea is generally safe, be cautious of narrow, winding roads, especially in mountainous areas. Always drive at a safe speed and remain alert for pedestrians, cyclists, and local traffic.
- **Speed Limits**: Speed limits are generally 50 km/h in towns and 80 km/h on highways, though these can vary, so watch for signs.
- Always ensure your rental car has insurance in case of accidents or damage.

Cycling Safety:

- Wear a helmet when cycling, as roads may be narrow and traffic can sometimes be heavy, particularly around Pape'ete.
- Carry a bottle of water and keep your phone charged for emergencies.

Wildlife and Nature Exploration:

- **Respect nature**: Leave wildlife and plants undisturbed. Do not approach animals or try to touch unfamiliar plants.
- **Hiking Trails**: Many hiking trails in Tahiti and Moorea can be rugged, with steep climbs and muddy conditions. Wear sturdy shoes and bring plenty of water and snacks.

Natural Disasters

While the islands of Tahiti and French Polynesia are generally safe, it's essential to be prepared for potential natural disasters:

- **Earthquakes**: French Polynesia lies within the Ring of Fire, so earthquakes are possible. It's a good idea to familiarize yourself with earthquake safety procedures.
- **Cyclones**: Cyclones are rare but can occur between November and April. If traveling during this period, keep an eye on local weather reports and have a plan in place.
- **Tsunamis**: French Polynesia is prone to tsunamis due to its location in the Pacific Ocean. If you're on the coast and feel an earthquake, head to higher ground immediately.

General Safety Tips

- **Stay Hydrated**: The tropical climate can be hot and humid, so always carry a water bottle and drink frequently.

- **Sunburn Protection**: Protect your skin from the sun using sunscreen, and avoid the hottest hours between 10 AM and 4 PM.
- **Personal Security**: While Tahiti and Moorea are generally safe, take the usual precautions:
    - Avoid walking alone at night in unfamiliar areas.
    - Keep your valuables, including passports and credit cards, in a safe place.
    - Be cautious of scams or overcharging, particularly in more tourist-heavy areas.

Chapter 10. Day Trips and Excursions

Exploring Neighboring Islands

Exploring Neighboring Islands in French Polynesia

French Polynesia is made up of over 100 islands, each with its own charm and unique appeal. While Tahiti is the most famous and well-known destination, the neighboring islands offer just as much to explore. Whether you're seeking untouched natural beauty, quiet retreats, or vibrant cultural experiences, these neighboring islands provide the perfect opportunity to broaden your adventure in French Polynesia.

Bora Bora

What to Expect:

- Bora Bora is renowned for its crystal-clear lagoon, stunning coral reefs, and luxury overwater bungalows. Known as the "Pearl of the Pacific," it is famous for its postcard-perfect views, with the Mount Otemanu (the highest point) towering over the island's turquoise waters.
- **Activities**: Snorkeling, diving, lagoon tours, and hiking are some of the most popular activities. Bora Bora also offers cultural experiences, including visits to local villages and historical sites.
- **Accessibility**: Bora Bora can be reached by a short flight (approx. 50 minutes) from Tahiti.

Cost: Luxury accommodations range from $400 per night, while more budget-friendly options are available starting at $150 per night.

Moorea

What to Expect:

- Located just a 30-minute ferry ride from Tahiti, Moorea is an island of lush, emerald-green mountains, pristine beaches, and shallow lagoons. Known for its beauty and tranquility, it offers a more laid-back atmosphere compared to Bora Bora.
- **Activities**: Hiking the Mount Rotui trail, visiting the Belvedere Lookout, exploring the island by bicycle or ATV, and snorkeling with rays and sharks in the lagoon. Moorea is also famous for its traditional Polynesian crafts, such as tahitian pearl jewelry and woven baskets.
- **Accessibility**: Moorea is just a short ferry ride from Pape'ete, Tahiti's capital. Flights are also available but not necessary for reaching the island.

Cost: Mid-range accommodations start from $150 per night, with more luxurious options available for upwards of $300.

Huahine

What to Expect:

- Often considered one of the more authentic islands in French Polynesia, Huahine is a haven for those seeking a quiet, less-touristy experience. It is known for its rich history, ancient Marae (temples), and beautiful lagoons surrounded by lush jungle.

- **Activities**: Exploring archaeological sites, hiking through the dense forests, and enjoying the secluded beaches. You can also rent a car or bicycle to explore the island at your own pace.
- Accessibility: Huahine can be reached by a 40-minute flight from Tahiti or by ferry (approximately 3 hours).

Cost: Budget-friendly options start from $100 per night, with mid-range stays averaging around $150–$200 per night.

Raiatea

What to Expect:

- Raiatea is one of the most significant islands in Polynesian culture, often referred to as the "sacred island" because of its historical and religious importance. With its lush valleys, flowing rivers, and towering mountains, Raiatea is perfect for nature lovers and cultural enthusiasts alike.
- **Activities**: Exploring ancient Marae temples, taking boat trips to the nearby Taha'a island (known for vanilla plantations), and hiking through dense forests. Raiatea is also a fantastic base for sailing or exploring nearby motus (small islets).
- **Accessibility**: A 50-minute flight from Tahiti gets you to Raiatea, which is a major hub for traveling to other islands in the region.

Cost: Budget accommodations start around $100, while mid-range hotels are priced from $150 to $250 per night.

Must-See Hidden Gems

French Polynesia is home to some of the world's most famous islands, but beyond the popular destinations like Bora Bora and Tahiti, there are lesser-known hidden gems waiting to be explored. These off-the-beaten-path locations offer a glimpse into the authentic beauty, culture, and history of the islands. From secluded beaches and untouched lagoons to ancient ruins and tranquil villages, the hidden gems of French Polynesia provide the perfect escape for those seeking adventure and serenity away from the crowds.

Bonus

Bonus: Simple Common Phrases To Help You Interact Like a Local

One of the highlights of traveling to French Polynesia is the chance to immerse yourself in the local culture, and learning a few simple phrases in Tahitian or French can go a long way in making connections with locals. This bonus section in the book offers a curated list of commonly used phrases that will help you interact smoothly with the Polynesian people. Whether you're ordering at a restaurant, asking for directions, or simply greeting someone, these phrases will make your experience more enjoyable and meaningful. Embracing the local language enhances your travel experience and helps foster a sense of respect and appreciation for the culture.

Tahitian Phrases:

- Ia ora na! – Hello! / Good day!
- 'O vai oe? – How are you?

- Ua ite au i te – I understand.
- E aha te huru? – How's it going?
- Noa oe? – Where are you from?
- Aita i te roaa – It's okay / No problem.
- Mauruuru – Thank you.
- Te ora na – Goodbye.
- Aita i maitai – It's not good.
- Ua here vau ia oe – I love you.
- No maita'i i teie nei – Very good now.
- E haere ana au – I am going.
- French Phrases:
- Bonjour! – Hello! / Good morning!
- Comment ça va? – How are you?
- Ça va bien, merci. – I'm fine, thank you.
- Où est...? – Where is...?
- Combien ça coûte? – How much does it cost?
- Je voudrais... – I would like...
- Merci beaucoup. – Thank you very much.
- Excusez-moi. – Excuse me.
- Parlez-vous anglais? – Do you speak English?
- Je ne parle pas bien français. – I don't speak French very well.
- Pouvez-vous m'aider? – Can you help me?
- Bonne journée! – Have a good day!

Useful website

Official Websites:

- **Tahiti Tourisme**
  Website: www.tahititourisme.org
  Information on activities, accommodations, and travel tips for all islands in French Polynesia.
- **Air Tahiti**
  Website: www.airtahiti.com
  Official airline of French Polynesia offering domestic flights between islands. Provides timetables, booking, and updates.
- **Air Tahiti Nui**
  Website: www.airtahitinui.com
  International airline flying to and from Tahiti, with routes from North America, Europe, and Asia.
- **French Polynesia Government Tourism Office**
  Website: www.polynesie-francaise.gov.pf
  Provides official information on government services, regulations, and tourism details in French Polynesia.

- **Transportation:**
- **Tahiti Ferry Services (Aremiti) Website**: www.aremiti.com
  Offers ferry services between Tahiti, Moorea, and other islands, with schedules and ticket booking.

- **Transports Polynésiens (Buses and Ferries) Website**: www.tp-pf.pf
  Information on bus routes and ferry services in Tahiti and the surrounding islands.
- **Le Truck – Public Bus Service (Tahiti) Website**: www.lettruck.pf
  Provides public bus services in Tahiti, with routes to popular destinations.

Emergency Contacts:

- **Police (Tahiti and French Polynesia) Phone**: +689 40 43 06 07
  Website: www.police.pf
  For emergency assistance and reporting incidents.
- **Ambulance Service Phone**: +689 15 15
  For medical emergencies, this number connects you to ambulance services.
- **Hospital (Tahiti) – Centre Hospitalier de Polynésie Française Phone**: +689 40 46 10 00
  Website: www.chpf.pf
  For healthcare services and medical support.
- **Tourism Police (Tahiti) Phone**: +689 40 50 82 20
  For assistance with travel-related issues, including lost property or travel disruptions.

Tourist Information Centers:

- **Tahiti Tourism Office (Papeete) Address**: Papeete, Tahiti
  Phone: +689 40 50 14 30
  Website: www.tahititourisme.org
  Provides information on things to do, attractions, and local advice.
- **Moorea Tourism Office Phone**: +689 40 56 70 05
  Website: www.moorea-tourism.com
  Offers information on Moorea Island, activities, accommodation, and tours.

Currency Exchange and Banking:

- **Banque de Polynésie Website**: www.banque-polynesie.pf
  Provides financial services, currency exchange, and ATM locations throughout French Polynesia.
- **Société Générale de Polynésie Website**: www.sgpf.pf
  Offers banking services, including currency exchange and international banking.

Additional Useful Resources:

- **Travel Insurance Website**: www.worldnomads.com
  Provides travel insurance options tailored to those visiting French Polynesia.
- **The Brando (Eco-Resort) Website**: www.thebrando.com
  A luxury eco-resort in French Polynesia. Offers bookings, information about sustainability, and visitor resources.
- **TripAdvisor Website**: www.tripadvisor.com
  Offers reviews, recommendations, and booking options for accommodations, restaurants, and

activities in French Polynesia.

A Heartfelt Request for Your Feedback and Review

Dear reader,

I hope this travel guide has been a valuable resource for you, whether you're planning an unforgettable vacation to Tahiti & French Polynesia or simply dreaming of the islands' beauty. Writing this book has been more than just a professional endeavor for me—it's been a deeply personal journey. It's a journey that involved not only extensive research but also an investment of my time, resources, and heart.

The insights and tips shared in this guide were shaped by my firsthand experiences exploring the stunning beaches, rich culture, and unique landscapes of these islands. I traveled to Tahiti and its neighboring islands with one goal in mind: to provide you with the most accurate, helpful, and up-to-date information that will allow you to fully experience the magic of French Polynesia.

As a travel guide writer, your feedback is invaluable. Your positive review and honest comments don't just help me improve— they help me continue this journey and grow in my craft. Writing a guidebook requires dedication and hard work, and it would mean the world to me if you could take a moment to share your thoughts. Your review not only supports me as a writer but also helps other travelers discover the treasures of French Polynesia.

The resources I've invested—both in terms of time and money—have been used to gather essential insights and experiences that you can now access in one place. Your feedback will fuel my future projects and encourage me to continue sharing the beauty of our world through detailed, passionate travel writing.

Thank you so much for trusting this guide to help shape your adventure. I truly hope it has inspired you and that you have an incredible time discovering everything Tahiti & French Polynesia has to offer. Please share your thoughts, as they are the foundation upon which my journey as a writer will continue to flourish.

Warm regards,

Pamala Whitney

Made in the USA
Monee, IL
07 March 2025